THE KINGIS QUAIR:

TOGETHER WITH

A BALLAD OF GOOD COUNSEL:

BY

KING JAMES I. OF SCOTLAND.

EDITED BY THE

REV. WALTER W. SKEAT, M.A.

ELRINGTON AND BOSWORTH PROFESSOR OF ANGLO-SAXON,
AND FELLOW OF CHRIST'S COLLEGE, CAMBRIDGE.

Published for the Society by

WILLIAM BLACKWOOD AND SONS
EDINBURGH AND LONDON
MDCCCLXXXIV

CONTENTS.

INTRODUCTION.

§ 1. It is not my intention to say much here concerning the royal author of the Kingis Quair, as accounts of him are easily accessible. In particular, I would refer the reader to the excellent sketch of the life of James I. in chap. vi. of The History of Scotish Poetry by David Irving; and to the account in Morley's English Writers, vol. ii. part I, p. 445, which is partly taken from Burton's History of Scotland. See also the Life of James I. in the editions of the Kingis Quair by Tytler and Chalmers, and The Life and Death of King James of Scotland, edited for the Maitland Club by Mr Stevenson in 1857.

§ 2. The facts of his life that immediately concern the reader of his chief poem may be briefly enumerated. He was born in July 1394, being the second son of King Robert III. and his queen Annabella Drummond.[1] The readers of Sir Walter Scott's 'Fair Maid of Perth' will remember the sad story of the cruel death of James's elder brother, the Duke of Rothsay, a circumstance which determined the king to send his remaining son to France, ostensibly for education, but really with a view to his safety. Accordingly, in the month of March 1405, Sir David Fleming, the king's kinsman, conducted the young prince

[1] Life by Chalmers, in 'Poetic Remains of the Scotish Kings,' p. 1.

to the Bass Rock, in the Firth of Forth, there to await the ship from Leith which was to carry him to France. As Sir David Fleming was returning to Edinburgh after taking leave of the prince, he was waylaid and slain. Shortly afterwards, the ship arrived, and the prince went on board with his tutor and companions. The ship was attacked by an English vessel off Flamborough Head in a time of truce, and, in defiance of all right and justice, James was taken prisoner, carried to Henry IV. at Windsor, and detained in England for many years. It is singular that the various accounts do not seem to be accurate in every particular. Thus Professor Morley speaks of the prince as being "a boy of fourteen," when it is quite certain that his age, in March 1405, was ten years and about eight months. Again, the date usually assigned for the prince's capture is the 12th of April 1405, being Palm Sunday; but in The Annals of England, 1876, p. 221, the date assigned is the 30th of March. There is even a doubt as to whether the ship was attacked in the open sea, or upon its venturing to approach the shore. These are questions of some interest, because James himself has something to say regarding them. In st. 22, he tells us he had passed "the state of innocence," i.e. seven years,[1] by the number of three years, so that he was over ten years old. As to the date of his embarkation, he is also explicit. In st. 21 and 22, he tells us that he "took his adventure to pass by sea out of his country, when the sun was beginning his course in Aries, and when it was four degrees past midday." He probably here refers to his first brief experience of the sea in passing by boat from North Berwick to the Bass Rock; a circumstance which impressed his mind so vividly that he

[1] See the note to st. 23.

was able to remember, years afterwards, that he entered the
boat at one o'clock on the 12th of March, being the day
when the sun entered the sign of Aries.[1] In st. 23, he
tells us that, when the ship was purveyed with all neces-
saries, and the wind was favourable, he and his companions
entered the ship *early in the morning*, and after many fare-
wells and expressions of good wishes for their safe journey
from those whom they left behind, they pulled up sail and
went forth upon their way. In st. 24, he expressly says
that his ship was attacked *at sea*, and soon overpowered, so
that he was taken prisoner by the strong hand, or to speak
it briefly, by force.

§ 3. It is certain that James derived many advantages
from his long captivity, and his tutor was allowed to take
much pains with his education, notwithstanding that he was
kept in strict confinement, at first in the Tower of London,
next at Nottingham, again in the Tower, and finally in the
Castle of Windsor.[2] All that James tells us about this time
is in st. 25, where he remarks that his captivity lasted
for nearly eighteen years, when he at last received comfort
by the first sight of the beautiful lady whom he afterwards
made his queen. He first saw her, just as Palamon and
Arcite first saw Emelye, as he was looking out from a
window in the castle into the castle-garden below; and his
description of her, and of his own feelings towards her, is
given in a well-known passage (st. 40 to 50), which has
been frequently admired. The lady was Johanne (or Joan)
Beaufort, daughter of the Earl of Somerset and Margaret
Holand; and it is even probable that there is a punning

[1] See Chaucer's treatise on the Astrolabe, ed. Skeat, part 2, sect. 1.
[2] See the account by Irving, and the extracts from Rymer's Fœdera (tom. 8,
p. 484, tom. 9, p. 2, tom. 9, p. 44) in Tytler's edition, p. 70.

allusion to her name in st. 47, where the poet mentions
the "floure-jonettis." This fortunate attachment was at
once encouraged, in the hope of gaining over the Scottish
prince to English interests, and was soon reciprocated by
the object of his affections, as we clearly learn from stanza
187, and he was at once allowed a much larger degree
of liberty, as he acknowledges in st. 181. Accordingly,
early in the following year, on the 2d of February 1424,
the young lovers were married in the Church of St Mary
Overy, and kept their wedding-feast in the Bishop of Win-
chester's palace, which was near at hand.[1] Arrangements
for his return to Scotland, upon payment of a ransom, were
soon made, so that he returned to his native land in April
of the same year, and was crowned King of Scotland at
Scone on the 21st of May.

§ 4. The story of the remainder of his life belongs to
Scottish history, though there is one more point of supreme
interest for all readers, namely, the dreadful narrative of his
barbarous assassination at Perth, on the 20th of February
1437. "He was at the close of the day" (says Professor
Morley) "loosely robed, chatting before the fire of the recep-
tion-room of the queen and her ladies. Three hundred
Highlanders, with Graham at their head, broke that night
into the monastery [of the Black Friars]. Bolts and locks
had been tampered with. It was then that Catharine
Douglas, finding that the great bolt of the chamber-door
had been removed, thrust her arm through the staples,
and suffered it to be crushed while time was gained for the
king's escape into a sewer-vault below. The flooring was
replaced, and the Highlanders, not finding the king, would

---

[1] Chron. of London from 1089 to 1483, London, 1827, p. 112; Stow's
Annales, London, 1615, p. 364; Fabyan's Chronicle, ed. 1811, p. 593.

have retired, but one who suspected the way of escape
caused the floor to be searched. James I. was discovered,
and was killed by sixteen wounds in the breast alone. Although unarmed, he defended himself well, leaving the mark
of his grip on those of his murderers with whom he grappled.
His wife, who sought to shelter him, was wounded in the
struggle." Such was the sad ending of a love so happily
begun.

§ 5. I have already said that the poem of the Kingis
Quair, that is, of the King's Book, was composed in 1423.
I do not find that it has been observed that we can date it
much more exactly than this. A careful study of the poem
has led me to believe that it was probably not composed
quite all at once; indeed, a poem of 1379 lines must have
occupied several days at least, and even at the rate of fifty
lines a-day, would have taken up nearly a month. We
find, accordingly, that the earlier part of the poem dwells
upon the king's state of despondency in the days preceding
the month of May, in which he first saw the lady Joan,
whilst the closing stanzas refer to a later period. Perhaps
we may date its commencement as early as April or March,
and its completion, probably, not earlier than June. We
also gain some insight into the manner of its composition.
It would seem probable that the poem was originally
begun as an amusement only, with the avowed hope of
beguiling his captivity; he lay awake in bed, thinking *of
this and that* (not, at this date, of his lady), and, finding
sleep impossible, began to read the treatise of Boethius De
Consolatione Philosophiæ ; he became interested in it (st. 5),
and, after shutting it up, continued to think of the variations of Fortune (st. 8). St. 11 follows naturally upon st.
9, and I am inclined to think that st. 10, in which he speaks

of Fortune being "afterwards his *friend*," was interpolated somewhat later. He had, at this time, no very clear idea as to what he was going to write about; he had, indeed, wasted much ink and paper to little effect (st. 13); but, being now ambitious to write "some new thing," and knowing that the best thing to do is to make a good beginning, he made a cross, and so began his book (st. 13). He still bewails his fate, and compares himself to a rudderless ship, since he has no object in life; nothing whereby to guide his voyage (st. 15); so that the poem probably made at first but little progress. St. 19, in which he mentions his torment and his *joy*, may have been slightly altered afterwards; for he seems to have begun his poem by determining to tell the story of his life and lamenting his fate, which continues till st. 28. But in st. 29 there is a great change; he had been bewailing his long days and nights for some time, and I suppose that st. 1 to 28 represent some of his reflections during this period. All at once a new note is struck, one of hope; he now no longer drifts about, but sets to his self-imposed task in good earnest, having found something definite to say; and it is not without some significance that the favourite extract from the poem begins with the thirtieth stanza.

§ 6. I do not find that any one has noticed a curious expression in st. 191. The lines to which I allude are the third and fourth of that stanza :—

> "Thankit mot be the sanctis marciall,
> That me first causit hath this accident."

For *marciall*, the editions by Tytler and others have *merciall*, and there is no note upon the line; nor does the word appear in Thomson's glossary, so that this interesting point has been missed. The "Martial saints" are the saints of

the month of Mars, *i.e.* of March ; and the poet blesses all
the saints of this happy month, because it " first caused him
this accident," *i.e.* was the *original cause* of his good fortune. I take this to refer, not to his first sight of his lady
(which certainly took place in *May*, as we learn expressly
from st. 34, 49, and 65), but to the month in which he first
quitted his native land ; and I think it highly probable
that the recurrence of the 12th of March—the anniversary
of the day when he first left home, and all his troubles
began (see st. 20)—caused him to turn his thoughts upon
the events of his past life. Moreover, it was this retrospect
which at last guided him to his new happiness; for it
was when he was tired of thinking that he went to the
window to seek for rest, or a fresh inspiration (st. 30),
and so beheld the garden and the lady. It is further
clear that the composition of the poem must have lasted
into June, since, after seeing the lady Joan in May, he
speaks of his hopes increasing " day by day " (st. 181),
of his " long pain and true service in love " (st. 188),
which led to his love being reciprocated,—of his " long
and true continuance in love and true service " (st. 192),
and of his further success in love " day by day " (st. 193).
Indeed, if we are to take the words in the *literal* sense, we
should have to allow even a still later date for the latter
portion of the poem ; but perhaps a month or six weeks
may fairly be considered a long term of service to a lover
who is anxious for the success of his suit. I think it will
also appear, upon examination, that the poem may have
been intended, at one time, to end with st. 173, which
is a sort of Envoy following upon st. 172, where he represents himself as awaking from his dream. I conclude
that the poem, or at any rate the first draft of it, was

begun at a time, when the poet had little to speak of beyond his past misadventures,—though it is very possible
that it was afterwards partially rewritten, owing to the
fresh impulse which was given to his fancy on a certain
May morning, and that it can hardly have been completed
till June.

§ 7. I believe that this hypothesis is also required by
the fragmentary nature of the poem ; for, notwithstanding
that some art has been shown in giving a certain connected-
ness to the whole by (as I suppose) the subsequent introduction of occasional connecting phrases, some want of
order still remains. The account of Fortune, in st. 158
to 172 with the addition of st. 173, is in a tone in harmony with st. 1 to 28, and might very well have been
introduced at an earlier place ; whilst st. 152 to 157 have
absolutely nothing to do with the subject, and have very
much the appearance of having formerly belonged to one
of the poet's earlier compositions, over which he spent,
as he tells us, so much paper and ink to so little effect.
The following very brief abstract of the poem will assist the
reader to form a judgment on this matter.

§ 8. The poet is lying awake at midnight, and being
unable to sleep, reads a portion of the treatise of Boethius
(1-7). Shutting the book, he meditates on reverses of fortune, till he hears the bell ring for matins (8-11). He at
once determines to write a new poem, and begins it with an
account of his state of doubt, misery, and uncertainty (12-
18). After invoking the muses, he begins the account of
the chief events of his youth, his departure from home, his
capture at sea, and his imprisonment in England (19-28).
To divert his thoughts, he walks to the window. This is
the turning-point of his life, for he hears in the garden
below the cheery songs of the nightingale, and presently

sees the lady Joan, who inspires him with love at first
sight, and whose person and dress he describes (29-50).
He addresses a stanza of praise to Venus, and implores the
nightingale to sing yet more sweetly (51-62). He next
addresses, in imagination, his lady, and the birds break out
into a happy chorus; but at this moment the lady departs,
and his day is turned into night (63-67). He mourns her
departure till even, when he falls asleep and dreams (68-73).
In his dream he sees a great light; he is carried up in the
air to the palace of Venus, where he sees a large chamber
filled with lovers of all ages and conditions (74-93).' He
also sees Cupid and the goddess Venus herself, whom he
salutes, praying her to grant him a second sight of his lady
(94-104). She promises her help, but tells him that the
success of his suit is uncertain, and that he must also seek
the help of Minerva (105-112). She sends Good Hope to
guide him to that goddess, at the same time lamenting that
mortals have lately become very slack in their service to
herself (113-123). Guided by Good Hope, he reaches the
palace of Minerva, who tells him that his love will be in
vain, unless it is firmly founded upon virtue; he must be
true and patient, and must confess to her the nature of his
love (124-138). He declares the truth of his passion, where-
upon she promises her help, not without some remarks on
the difficult questions of predestination and free-will (139-
150). She then dismisses him, and he suddenly returns to
earth (151). He now sees a plain, a river full of fishes, and
a long row of trees; also an assemblage of numerous wild
and tame animals (152-157). He quits the plain, searching
for the goddess Fortune, when suddenly his former guide,
Good Hope, appears and shows him a round space walled
in, within which is Fortune, dressed in a long ermine mantle;
before her is a wheel, ever revolving, upon which men are

constantly clambering, some of whom frequently fall off into
a pit below (158-165). Fortune calls him by name, leads
him to her wheel, and bids him climb upon it like the rest
(166-171). She then bids him farewell; he awakes, and
addresses his own spirit in a stanza imitated from Chaucer
(172, 173). The poem is here rather inartistically continued
by his reflections upon the meaning of the dream, and by
the sudden appearance of a white turtle-dove, who brings a
branch, on which is written a message of encouragement
(174-179). Thus encouraged, he urges his suit, and is
successful, concluding the poem with a prayer to Venus,
thanks to all the gods, to Fortune, to the nightingale, to the
window in the castle-wall, and to all the saints of March,
as having contributed to his good fortune (180-193). Then
follows the Envoy, with an address to the poems of Chaucer
and Gower (194-197).

§ 9. Perhaps this is the most convenient place for explaining the method of reference employed in the present
edition. The poem is written continuously in the MS., and
I have accordingly numbered the stanzas throughout continuously, from 1 to 197. It pleased Tytler, who first
edited the poem in 1783, to divide it into six imaginary
cantos; and his method of division has been followed by
nearly all his successors (who, for the most part, only knew
the text from his book). This explains why the references
in Jamieson's Dictionary are to cantos and stanzas. To
understand Tytler's numbering, all that is necessary is to
note where his cantos begin. His canto ii. begins with st.
20; canto iii., with st. 74; canto iv., with st. 124; canto v.,
with st. 152; and canto vi., with st. 173. Hence we must
add 19 to the number of his stanza throughout canto ii.;
and so on throughout, as in the following table :—

Throughout canto ii., add the number 19
    ,,   ,, iii., ,,   ,,   73
    ,,   ,, iv., ,,   ,,   123
    ,,   ,, v., ,,   ,,   151
    ,,   ,, vi., ,,   ,,   172

For example : Jamieson quotes the word *amorettis* as occurring in c. ii. st. 28 ; it therefore occurs in st. 47. Conversely,
by *subtracting* 19, we find that st. 47 is called by Tytler
c. ii. st. 28.

§ 10. I pass on to consider what we know of other poems
by the same author. I have printed, at p. 51, a Ballad of
which the authenticity is unquestionable. It is ascribed to
James I. in an early printed edition, and the internal evidence points the same way; see the Notes upon the Ballad
at p. 94. With this exception, I contend that we have no
other poem extant which can be attributed to him with any
show of reason, and I entirely decline to follow the critics
who ascribe to him the ' Song on Absence,' or ' Peebles to
the Play,' or 'Christ's Kirk on the Green.' Of these three,
the first is the only one that, in my opinion, can even
possibly be his, if the internal evidence is at all to be
regarded. It is a song in 13 stanzas, the first of which is
as follows, according to the version in Pinkerton's Ancient
Scotish Poems, 1786, ii. 214 :—

> " Sen that [the] eyne, that workis my weilfair
>   Dois no moir on me glance,
> A thousand sichis, with suelting sobbis sair,
>   Dois throw my bowels lance.
>   I die yairning ;
>   I leif pyning ;
>   Woe dois encres ;
>   I wex witles ;
>   O sindering, O woful doleance ! "

But Pinkerton proposes to alter the first line in order to
force it into agreement with the supposed evidence. He
himself admits that, in the Maitland MS. in the Pepysian
Library, which is the original which he professes to follow,
it really stands thus—

> " Sen that eyne that workis my weilfair."

But he assumes that the line is " mutilated," for the following reason. In Mair's History of Scotland, we find the
following remarks, as quoted by Irving, Lives of the Scotish Poets, p. 144. They refer to King James I. "In
vernacula lingua artificiosissimus compositor: cujus codices
plurimi et cantilenæ memoriter adhuc apud Scotos inter
primos habentur. Artificiosum libellum de regina dum
captivus erat composuit, antequam eam in conjugem
duceret ; et aliam artificiosam cantilenam ejusdem, *Yas sen*,
etc. et jucundum artificiosumque illum cantum *At Beltayn*,
etc. quem alii de Dalketh et Gargeil mutare studuerunt :
quia in arce aut camera clausus servabatur in qua mulier
cum matre habitabat."—Major, De Gestis Scotorum, fol.
cxxxv a., Paris, 1521, 4to. All admit that the *artificiosus
libellus de regina* is certainly the Kingis Quair ; the next
endeavour of the critics was to find the song beginning
with *Yas sen*, or the poem beginning with *At Beltayn*.
Now it should have been observed at the outset that Mair
(or his printer) seems to have made a mistake ; for the
words *Yas sen* give no sense, and there is indeed no such
word as *Yas*. Pinkerton was probably thinking of *yes*, but
this in Scottish would be spelt *ȝis*, as in Barbour, or *ȝus ;*
and, since the symbol ȝ was denoted in print by *z*, it would
have appeared as *Zis*. Hence Mair's evidence is not of
much help, and certainly Pinkerton was not justified in

supposing that he had found the song intended because he found one beginning with the word *Sen.* In fact, it is not a little remarkable that the Ballad, which we know to be genuine, also begins with the same word! Hence there is absolutely *no* evidence in favour of attributing to King James this Song on Absence. It is a pleasing poem, and not foreign to the style of the Kingis Quair; the *language* is, perhaps, sufficiently archaic, but I am by no means sure that the same can be said of the *metre.* On the whole, I could find nothing to justify its insertion in the present volume.

§ 11. It remained for the critics to find the poem beginning with the words *At Beltayn.* This they discovered in the poem known as Peebles to the Play, which actually begins with those words. The first stanza is thus printed in Sibbald's Chronicle of Scottish Poetry, vol. i. p. 121, the original being contained in the Maitland MS. already mentioned :—

> "At Beltane, quhen ilk bodie bownis
>   To Peblis to the Play,
> To heir the singin and the soundis,[1]
>   The solace, suth to say;
> Be firth and forrest furth they found,
>   Thay graythit tham full gay;
> God wait that wald they do that stound,
>   For it was their feist day,
>   Thai said,
> Of Peblis to the play."

Now the testimony of Mair tells almost as much *against* the authenticity of this poem as in its favour. James's poem, he says, was not to be got at, but was kept somewhere in safe custody; on which account others of " Dalketh and

---

[1] Read *sounis*, the correct form.

Gargeil" endeavoured to write substitutes for it, and of
course would begin with the two words by which it seems
to have been known. This is what I understand by Mair's
remark, taking *cantus* as the implied nominative case to
servabatur, in opposition to Sibbald's remark that " the occasion or subject of the parodies was *by reason of his having been shut up in a tower or chamber in which a woman
resided with her mother.*" However this may be, we find
that there was more than one *imitation* of James's poem, so
that Peebles to the Play, as now known to us, is more likely
to have been one of these imitations than the original. If, for
example, there were but two imitations, the chances of its
being one of these, as against its being the original, are
obviously as two to one. The moment we come to examine
the poem itself, the notion of attributing it to James I.
seems to me entirely out of the question ; I cannot even
admit that it is an imitation made during his reign, and it
must be remembered that Mair did not write till the sixteenth century, and says nothing about the *date* of these
imitations. In fact, his testimony is almost worthless at
best, the only surprising point being that he is right as to
the Kingis Quair itself. For it is very remarkable that
Dunbar, in his Lament for the Death of the Makars, *i.e.* of
the Poets, does not even mention James I. by name, though
he enumerates the names of no less than twenty-three
Scottish poets, and includes among them such names as
Wyntoun, Holland, Barbour, and Blind Harry. The
question of the authorship of Peebles to the Play has been
discussed almost *ad nauseam ;* but the internal evidence
ought to decide the matter. There is no resemblance to
the Kingis Quair discoverable ; whereas there is a marked
dissimilarity in the tone, in the vocabulary, and in the

metre. It will be found by no means easy to point out any undoubted example of the use of the rollicking metre of this poem anterior to the year 1450; whereas James I. died in 1437. The burden of proof lies upon those who think they can meet all the objections arising from the obvious lateness of its style and metre.[1]

§ 12. But the critics have not been contented to stop here. It so happens that another poem, entitled Christ's Kirk on the Green (printed together with Tytler's edition of the Kingis Quair, and in Sibbald's Chron. of Scot. Poetry, ii. 359), is ascribed to James the First in the Bannatyne MS. by a probable blunder for James the Fift (Fifth), to whom it has also been assigned, viz. by Bp. Gibson in 1691, by James Watson in 1706, and by others. It is necessary to quote (from Sibbald) the first stanza :—

> "Was nevir in Scotland hard nor sene
>   Sic dansing nor deray,
>   Nowthir at Falkland on the grene,
>   *Nor Pebillis at the play*,
>   As wes of wowaris, as I wene,
>   At Chryst-kirk on ane day.
>   There come our Kitteis weschin clene,
>   In new kirtillis of gray,
>   Full gay,
>   At Chrystis kirk on the grene."

The reader will at once observe the mention, in the fourth line, of Peebles to the Play, as if that poem was still fresh in the recollection of every reader of Christ's Kirk. He should also observe the exact correspondence in metre (and, it might be added, in tone) with that poem. The natural conclusion is that they are of the same age. But we can go further, and discover to what

---

[1] In st. 19, we find *stokks* rimed with *ox*. But with James I., the plural of *stok* was *stokkis*.

age Christ's Kirk belongs; for Sibbald has pointed out the very close verbal resemblance between Christ's Kirk and a poem called the Justing of Barbour and Watson, by Sir David Lyndsay. The latter poem, printed among Lyndsay's Minor Poems,[1] ed. J. A. H. Murray, E.E.T.S., p. 585, begins in a very similar strain :—

> "In Sanctandrois on Witsoun Monnunday . . . .
> Was neuer sene sic Iusting in no landis."

And below we have the lines :—

> "Quod Iohne, howbeit thou thinkis my leggis lyke rokkis . . . .
> ȝit, thocht thy braunis be lyk twa barrow-trammis,
> Defend the, man ! Than ran thay to, lyk rammis."

These lines are to be compared with the following lines in Christ's Kirk :—

> "His lymmis wer lyk twa rokkis . . . .
> Ran apoun uder lyk rammis . . . .
> Bet on with barrow-trammis."

The obvious conclusion is that Christ's Kirk belongs to the reign of James V., though I doubt if it was composed by him. And, in claiming this poem for James I., certain critics have claimed too much. It may be granted that Peebles to the Play and Christ's Kirk are in the same peculiar metre and nearly of the same date, but the safest result is to assign Peebles to the Play to the sixteenth century. In accordance with this, it may be mentioned that the earliest mention of Christ's Kirk is that by Bannatyne, in 1568; and the earliest *certain* mention of Peebles to the Play is in the poem of Christ's Kirk, as above. If we are to have any regard at all to the language, style, and metre of these poems, we cannot make them earlier

---

[1] An early edition was printed at Edinburgh in 1568.

than half a century or more after 1437. The case is precisely parallel to the assignment to Chaucer of the poem called the Court of Love, which no philologist can admit to be earlier than the close of the fifteenth century. It is needless to pursue the subject further; for no arguments will ever convince those who have adopted a notion of the antiquity of these poems, whilst those who perceive their lateness require no further argument.[1]

§ 13. The consideration of the style of these poems naturally leads us to consider the language of the Kingis Quair, especially with regard to its grammatical forms. This is a point which has hitherto received no attention, whereas it evidently lies at the root of the whole matter. All that we have been told hitherto is that he was a close imitator of Chaucer, and the most explicit utterance upon this subject is contained in the following passage, which I cite from Mr T. H. Ward's remarks upon King James in his excellent edition of the English Poets, vol. i. p. 130: "His nineteen years of captivity allowed him to steep himself in Chaucer's poetry, and any Chaucerian student who reads The King's Quair is constantly arrested by a line or a stanza or a whole episode that exactly recalls the master. It is unnecessary to point out, for instance, the close resemblance of the passage which we here quote, the king's first sight of Lady Jane, to the passage in The Knightes Tale, where Palamon and Arcite first see Emilye. Not only the general idea but the details are copied; for example, the king, like Palamon, doubts whether the beautiful vision be woman or goddess. The ascent to the Empire of Venus is like an

[1] "One can hardly suppose those critics serious, who attribute this song [of Christ's Kirk] to the moral and sententious James the First."—Guest, Eng. Rhythms, ed. 1882, p. 624.

abridgment of The Hous of Fame. Minerva's discussion of Free Will is imitated from Chaucer's rendering of the same theme, after Boethius, in Troylus and Creseyde. The catalogue of beasts near the dwelling of Fortune, is an echo of Chaucer's catalogue of birds in The Parlement of Foules. Isolated instances of imitation abound ; thus :—

> 'Til Phebus endit had his bemës brycht,
>   And bad go farewele every leef and floure,
>   That is to say, approchen gan the nyght,'

is a repetition of a well-known passage in The Frankeleynes Tale :—

> 'For the orizont had reft the sonne his lyght,
>   (This is as much to seyn as it was nyght).'

A passage in Troylus is recalled by—

> 'O besy gost, ay flikering to and fro ;'

and another by the king's concluding address to his book— 'Go, litel tretis.'"

§ 14. It will be seen that Mr Ward here points out about eight examples of resemblance between the language of James and of Chaucer, which were quite sufficient for his purpose. But I have thought it desirable to make a much stricter search, for the results of which I must refer the reader to the Notes. I find clear allusions to, or phrases copied from, the following poems by Chaucer: Troilus and Cressida, the metre of which is imitated, which furnishes more than a dozen instances; The Knightes Tale, with at least as many; The Clerkes Tale, with two instances; other of the Canterbury Tales; the Book of the Duchess; Annelida and Arcite; the Assembly of Foules; the Complaint of Mars; Lenvoy a Skogan; the Legend of Good Women; and probably (as Mr Ward says) the House of Fame. To take a few examples that have not hitherto been noticed, we may observe how close is the resemblance in the following instances :—

> " Streight vnto schip, no longere wold we tarye."—K. Q. 23.
> "And forth he goth, no longer wolde he tarye."—C. T. 12,785.
> " Paciently thou tak thyne auenture."—K. Q. 106.
> " And patiently takth your auenture."—Compl. of Mars, 21.
> " All thing has time, thus sais Ecclesiaste."—K. Q. 133.
> " For alle thing hath time, as sayn thise clerkes."—C. T. 9846.
> " Has maist in mynde : I can say 30u no more."—K. Q. 182.
> " And liuen in wele; I can seye you no more."—C. T. 4595.
> " Quho couth it red, agone syne mony a 3ere."—K. Q. 196.
> " Is writen, god wot, who so coude it rede."—C. T. 4615.
> " But soth is said, gon sithen are many yeres."—C. T. 1523.

It is needless to cite more examples; but I may add that, over and above the allusions to Chaucer, we find that the poet refers to the Latin treatise of Boethius and to Le Roman de la Rose.

§ 15. But it is not sufficient to consider these direct imitations of Chaucer; we must go a step further, and enquire strictly into the *grammar* which our author employs. We are at once met by the startling fact, that he abandons the grammar used in the Lowlands of Scotland, and attempts to imitate all the inflections of the Midland dialect of Chaucer, evidently considering him as furnishing the true model of literary form. Hence his poem is by no means, as has been supposed, an example of Northern English; it exhibits a purely *artificial* dialect, such as probably was never spoken. We have a precisely parallel example in the poem of Lancelot of the Laik, edited by me for the Early English Text Society in 1865, the author of which affects Southern forms to such an extent as to produce a curious jumble such as was never employed in actual speech.

Nothing could show more clearly the predominating influence, at this period, of Chaucer's genius. The result, by the way, is the more remarkable, because James was perfectly acquainted with the Lowland dialect. This is ascertained by the preservation of a most interesting document, entirely in the king's own handwriting, written at Croydon in 1412. It runs as follows : [1]—

"Jamis throu the grace of god . Kynge of Scottis. Til all that this lettre heris or seis sendis gretynge. Wit ƺe that we haue grauntit & be this presentis lettres grauntis . a speciall confirmaciun in the mast forme til oure traiste and wele belofit Cosyng sir William of Douglas of drumlangrig of all the landis that he is possessit . and charterit of within the kyngdome of Scotlande that is for to say the landis of drumlangrig of Hawyke & of Selkirke the whilkis charts & possiouns[1]. be this lettre we conferme . and wil for the mare sekernes this our confirmacioune . be formabilli efter the fourme of oure chaunssellare and the tenor of his chartris selit with oure grete sele in tyme to come in witnes of the whilkis this presentis lettres we wrate with oure propre hande vndir the signet vsit . in selyng of oure lettres as now at Croidoune the last dai of Nouember the ƺere of oure lorde . imo cccco xijo."

§ 16. In this document we have but little mixture of dialect. The verbs show the Northern suffix -is, both in the singular and in the plural, except that *conferme* should rather have been *confermis;* and the weak past participles show the Northern suffix -it. When we turn to the poem,

---

[1] A facsimile is given by Chalmers, and is the only thing of value in his worthless book, of which more below. Chalmers misprints *Till, al, daie,* for *Til, all,* and *dai.*

[2] *Sic;* for *possessiouns.* The facsimile is not quite accurate; it has *fouome* for *fourme,* and a few other dubious letters.

all this is changed; and it is evident, from the exigencies of
the metre, that the numerous Midland (or rather Southern)
inflections are due rather to the author than to the scribe.
As this can only be shown by a tolerably strict analysis of
the poem, I proceed to show this formally. The rules for
the scansion of Chaucer, in accordance with the grammatical forms employed by him, are given in the Introduction
to my edition of Chaucer's Prioresses Tale, 3d edition,
1880, pp. liv-lxxiv. I select some of the more important
rules, and give examples of them from our poem.[1]

(*a*) The infinitive mood in Chaucer ends in *-e* or *-en*, con-
stituting a syllable, though *-e* is elided before a following
vowel. The Northern infinitive and gerund admit of *no* suffix, so that *to smert* (8)[2] is correct and natural to the author.
But he has several examples of the artificial suffix *-e* or *-en*;
as in *wirken* (68), *seken* (99), *trusten* (137), *helpen* (144), *sup-
porten* (194). In these instances the scribe has correctly pre-
served the suffix, and we are hence enabled to correct the
instances wherein he has not done so, thus restoring the
correct scansion. Accordingly we must read *approchen* (72),
fallen (148), *clymben* (164, 169), *reulen* (194). Similarly, the
suffix *-e* appears in *change* (83), *deserue* (143); and must be
restored in *lette* (113). We find the suffix *-en* in the present
tense plural of the verb, as in *menen* (137); similarly we
should read *gruchen* (91). The Northern forms would be
menis, gruchis, but we may suspect that the scribe is right
here. A crucial instance occurs in st. 24, where *weren* is
dissyllabic, as in Chaucer; for the Northern form is *war*, as

---

[1] When the final *-e* forms a distinct syllable, I have denoted this in the text
by the use of a mark of diæresis, as in *estatë* in st. 3. In some doubtful cases
of final *-en* I have also marked the syllable, as in *eyën* in st. 41. So also *sterëles*
in st. 15 has three syllables.

[2] The number within a parenthesis is the number of the stanza.

in Barbour's Bruce, which should be consulted for information as to Northern grammar.

(*b*) A peculiarity of Chaucer is, that many words which are monosyllabic in Northern English are dissyllabic in Midland. An excellent example occurs in the word *heart*—Northern *hert*, Midland *herte*.[1] The king uses the Chaucerian form, though the scribe does not write it; in four instances it is written *hert*, where the metre requires *herte* (48, 128, 170, 177). In the last instance *kálendis* is almost dissyllabic, the final *-is* being slurred over before the following vowel. That the form *herte* was unnatural to the writer, appears from the use of *hertly*, not *hertely*, in st. 144. In st. 9 the scribe writes *estate*, where *estat* is meant, the word being dissyllabic; but the artificial trisyllabic form, *estate*, occurs in st. 3. Other artificial forms occur in the dissyllables *prynce* (9), *eye* (51), *wise*, *charge* (120), *gyde* (126), *lufe* (134), *chance* (146), *sonne* (153), *quhele* (162).

(*c*) Chaucer sometimes uses a final *-e* to denote the vocative case; the king imitates this in the word *suete* (57). This is not Northern.

(*d*) Chaucer uses a final *-e* to mark the plural of the adjective. Of this James has numerous instances, as in *grene* (33), *faire* (76), *fresche* (80), *huge* (100), *bothe* (124), *fresche* (152), *grene* (191). Hence we can confidently restore the metre in other instances by reading *ʒonge* (86, 92), *longe* (29, 95). So also, in the phrase *grete balas*, the form *balas* has a plural sense (46). *Foure* is dissyllabic, as in st. 21. These usages are not Northern.

(*e*) Chaucer uses a final *-e* to denote the *definite* form of the adjective, this use being determined by the occurrence

---

[1] To be read *hert-e*, in two syllables, the final *e* being sounded as in German. And so throughout, in all other instances.

of *the* or *that* or *this*, or of a possessive pronoun, before the adjective. This is not Northern; yet examples abound. Hence we find *his faire* (7), *the plane* (36), *hir suete* (41), *hir quhyte* (48), *that fresche* (49), *the suete* (61), *the suete grene,* where the adjectives are plural (67), *the hote* (76), *ȝour benigne* (102), *that suete* (103); and see stanzas 109, 130, 133, 143, (*this ilke*) 154, 155. Had the scribe understood this matter, there would have been more examples still; for we can restore the metre in numerous places by reading *the longe* (8), *the sharpe* (32), *the freschest ȝonge* (40), *thir calde* (69), *the longe* (72), *the colde* (73), *the ryghte* (75), *the nexte* (86), *the blynde* (94), *this faire* (178), *the faire* (191). Positive proof of the truth of this rule is afforded by such an example as that in st. 32, where we find: "The scharpë grenë suetë Ienepere." For here the omission of the final *e* would leave but seven syllables in the line, and would produce a most jarring discord, such as no man with an ear could have endured. The king's ear for melody was doubtless a fine one. So also in st. 33, we find: "And on the smallë grenë twistis sat."

(*f*) But here comes in a most curious result. Chaucer does *not*, in general, use the final *-e* in adjectives occurring in the singular and indefinitely. This is a refinement of grammar to which James did not attain. It is the fate of writers in an artificial dialect that they make mistakes of this character, just as Spenser has perpetrated some extraordinary offences against grammatical propriety in his Fairy Queen. Accordingly, we find the king wrongly adding a final *-e* to indefinite adjectives in several places; he seems to have regarded it as a poetical embellishment, to be added or dropped at pleasure, a theory which had doubtless great practical convenience. A clear instance of this false

usage occurs in st. 65, where we should read, "With new-e
fresch-e suete and tender grene"; the *e* in *suete* being elided
before the following vowel. Other examples are seen in
large (77), *strange* (135), *hye* (154), *strange* (163), *lawe* (164),
newe (165), *gude* (185). To these add *longe* (154), *faire* (178),
miswritten *long* and *fair* respectively. I think we should
also read *rounde* in st. 159, l. 2, to complete the line, but I
omitted to observe it soon enough to suggest it in the text.
It may be observed that the final *-e* is, however, permissible
in *some* of these words—viz., in the French words *large*,
strange, and in the word *newe*, which was naturally dissyllabic; but the forms *hye, lawe, gude, longe, faire*, as here
used, are hardly defensible. They are not only not Northern;
they are not even Chaucerian. The worst example of a
false concord occurs in the first line of st. 117: "And quhen
I wepe, and *stenten* othir quhile." It will be observed that
the form *stenten* is absolutely required for the scansion; yet
it is a *plural* form, just as if we should use the expression
ego amamus in writing Latin. Yet it is quite explicable;
it is a translation into Chaucerian language of the Northern
word *styntis*; for, in the Northern dialect, the phrases *I
stintis* and *we stintis* were once equally correct.

(*g*) Chaucer uses a final *e* to denote an adverbial use;
this is unknown to the Northern dialect. I do not find
many examples. Still we have *newe*, newly (8), *longe*, a
long while (164), *faire*, fairly (180). So also the adverbial
phrase *at the last* (98) is miswritten for *at the laste*, so commonly written *atte laste* in MSS. of Chaucer.

(*h*) Chaucer makes the adverb *twi-es* (twice) a dissyllable; accordingly, the scansion shows that *twise* in st. 25
is a mistake for *twies*; see the footnote.

(*i*) Chaucer makes the word *ey-en* (eyes) dissyllabic;

hence we find the same twice (8, 104). But in one instance our author is off his guard, using *eyne* (= *eyn*) in st. 35 ; probably because a vowel follows, and Chaucer sometimes slurs over the syllable -*en* before a vowel.

(*k*) Chaucer frequently has a syllabic *e* in the middle of a word ; an example occurs in *ster-e-les* (three syllables) in st. 15. This is hardly Northern ; but examples are rather numerous. We have *vnkynd-e-nes* (87, 116), *chap-el-let* (97), *benign-e-ly* (104), *pap-e-iay* (110), *diuers-e-ly* (135) ; so also we should read *hert-e-full* (180) ; *henn-es-furth* (69, 144, 181). The last word is miswritten in all three places. But occasionally the king forgets his master's rules, using *hertly* for *hert-e-ly* (144), *chaplet* for *chap-el-let* (46).

(*l*) Chaucer uses -*es*, forming a distinct syllable, to denote plurals. Here our author was quite at home, for the Northern dialect used -*is* (forming a distinct syllable) for the same purpose. Examples occur in *sterres* (1), *werdes* (9), *wawis* (16), *flouris* (21), &c. ; it is needless to add more examples. The same remark applies to the final -*es* (Northern -*is*), used to mark the genitive case. Examples are *warldis* (3), *goddis* (22), *lyvis* (28), &c. ; more need not be given. Hence we clearly see that the scribe should have written *rokkis* in st. 15, just as in st. 18.

(*m*) Chaucer distinguishes between the past tenses and past participles of some weak verbs by using a final *e* in the former, but none in the latter. Thus *bringen*, to bring, makes the past tense *broght-e*, but the pp. *broght ;* compare the usage of modern German. My experience tells me that this is the most difficult point in the scansion of Chaucer for a learner to realise, and I find no trace of it in the present poem. The Northern suffix -*it* was used for the past tense and past participle indifferently ; hence we find always *-ed* or *-it* or *-d* or *-t* in such cases. The scribe has miswritten *lak* for *lakit* (16); and the author slurs over the final syllables of *purvait* and *pullit* before following vowels in st. 23.

(*n*) In st. 34 I suspect the scribe has miswritten the first word, which is an instance of the imperative plural. Chaucer would have written *Worshippeth;* Northern grammar requires *Worshippis.* Either way, the word is trisyllabic, which is my reason for so marking it. In st. 117, *patience* has three syllables ; Chaucer assigns it four, as *pac-i-enc-e.*

§ 17. The preceding investigation is of the highest importance to the correction of the text; and the fact that no editor has ever hitherto made such an investigation explains why so little has been done for the text hitherto, and why the MS. copy has received so little attention. The net result is that the lines of James I., like the lines of Chaucer, are *beautifully musical,* and quite different from the halting lines of Lydgate. We now see that we have a right to expect that every line should be perfect, and should scan with exact regularity. Hence we can detect, in many places, the omission by the scribe of words and syllables that are necessary to the scansion ; and it at once appears that, in many instances, it is quite as necessary, for the *sense* as for the *metre,* that we should supply one or more words in a line. Words thus supplied are enclosed within square brackets, so that they can easily be considered. Easy and obvious examples occur in st. 3, l. 3 ; st. 8, l. 7 ; st. 16, l. 3 ; st. 20, l. 5 ; st. 28, l. 3 ; st. 52, l. 4, &c. The absolute necessity for supplying a final *e* in many places has been shown above, and may at once be understood in such a case as that of *scharpe* in st. 32.

When these corrections have been made, the number of

incomplete lines is very greatly reduced ; the principal ones being as follows :—

St. 1, l. 7.   Perhaps we should read *north-e-ward*, in three syllables.

St. 31, l. 6.   Perhaps we should read the artificial word *y-walking*.

St. 53, l. 4.   For *vnto* read *to*.

St. 74, l. 7.   A syllable too much.

St. 82, l. 3.   The same remark applies as in st. 31, l. 6 ; but it is not impossible that the cæsura (as it sometimes does) counts for a syllable.

St. 86, l. 6.   A syllable too much ; perhaps *sorouful*.

St. 97, l. 5.   A syllable too much.   Omit *that ;* the omission of the relative is common.

St. 110, l. 4.   Read *tabartis* as *tabarts ;* this use of *s* for final *-is* occurs occasionally, when a substantive has *more than one syllable*.   So also *kalendis*, st. 177, l. 7.

St. 158, l. 3.   Imperfect, either owing to the cæsura, or because *furth* is practically dissyllabic.

St. 159, l. 2.   Read *round-e*, dissyllabic.

St. 161, l. 1.   *Er-myn* seems to count as having three syllables.

For further information, as to elision, slurring, &c., the reader is referred to my remarks on Chaucer, already noticed above.

§ 18. The Ballad of Good Counsel is written in a pure Northern dialect, without a single example of a Southern form.   It has been shown (§ 15) that James could, upon occasion, write the Northern dialect purely, so that this circumstance furnishes no presumption against its authenticity.   The *style* is precisely that of the Kingis Quair, and I have no doubt that it should be accepted as being from

c

the same hand. The earliest MS. is of the end of the
fifteenth century.

§ 19. I have to add a final remark on the grammar. The
Northern writers who imitated Chaucer seem to have got
into trouble with the suffix *-ing*, or else the scribes did not
understand it. This is shown in my preface to Lancelot of
the Laik (Early English Text Society). Properly, the suffix
-ing denoted the present participle, or a substantive derived
from a verb; but it was confused with the Midland suffix
-en of the present indicative plural, and with the common
English suffix *-en* of the past participles of strong verbs.
Hence, in st. 1, l. 2, *twynklyng* appears to be for *twynklen*,
pres. pl. indicative. In st. 45, l. 4, *I-fallyng* stands for
I-fallen, the pp.; here the prefix *I-* is Southern, and unknown to Northern English. Yet it recurs in *Iblent* (74),
Ilokin (69), *Iwone* (108), *Ilaid* (120), &c., and was evidently
regarded as a poetical embellishment. We even find the
infinitive *ybete* (116). In st. 6 we find the Southern *makith*
(for *maketh*) instead of the Northern *makis*; but it is useless
to discuss such instances, as we are here at the mercy of the
scribe.

§ 20. The *rimes* are, I believe, *Northern* rimes throughout,
and mostly only single rimes, after the Northern fashion of
ignoring the final *-e*. We find words rimed together which
Chaucer never admitted; thus in st. 11 Chaucer would have
written *sodaynly*, which cannot be rimed with *ly-e, fantasy-e*;
nor does he rime *forby* with *remedy-e* (30), nor with *aspy-e*
(31); nor *louingly* with *maystry-e* (66), &c. The rimes are,
from the author's point of view, perfect, with the exception
of *corage*, which is not a perfect rime with *charge* and *large*
(38). In st. 39, *regne* is for *rigne* (Northern *ring*), and is
thus a permissible rime with *benigne*. In st. 7, *tong* is

repeated ; so is *mynd* in st. 73, and *fall* as a substantive is
rimed with *fall* as a verb in st. 172. In st. 92, the riming
of *dryue* with *gyue* is permissible, because *dryue* is the pp.,
and the *i* is short ; but the more correct form is *driuen*. Instances of true double rimes are very common, as in the
case of *deuidith*, *prouidith* (9). For other instances, see st.
6, 7, 14, 21, 23, 28, 47, 65, 68, 69, 79, 85, 90, 99, 105, 111, &c.

§ 21. I have been led into these details because it enables
me to explain more clearly the method which I have adopted in editing the poem. My first care was to set aside all
previous editions, and to obtain an accurate copy of the
MS. itself, which has been far too much neglected. It is an
amazing fact that it has taken *a whole century* to set the
text right, and nothing can be more extraordinary than the
history of the text up to the present time. The previous
editions are described more particularly below ; but the net
result is that Tytler, who first printed the text in 1783, was
provided with a transcript of the unique MS. made by " an
ingenious young gentleman, a student of Oxford " ; it does
not appear that he ever saw the MS. himself. Sibbald,
when reprinting a large portion of the poem, tells us that
his " is the first *corrected* copy." His notion of correcting
it was to make just a few alterations here and there, according to his own fancy. It does not appear that he ever saw
the MS., but some one must have consulted it for him, as
he attained to the correct reading of *list* for *lefe* in st. 178.
The Glasgow edition of 1825 is a reprint of Tytler. Chalmers, after severely censuring Tytler for his numerous errors,
actually sends Tytler's book to press, and copies text,[1] notes,
and all ; but he never saw the MS., and scarcely paid the
slightest heed to the collation made for him by Mr Ruding,

[1] In a sort of parody ; see below.

which, though not always correct, was better than nothing.
The Rev. C. Rogers, in 1873, merely collated the texts of
Tytler and Chalmers, which amounted to no more than
collating Tytler with Chalmers's parody of the same. The
only editor who ever saw the MS. himself, or paid any
regard to it, was Mr Ebenezer Thomson of Ayr; but he
did not make his collation till after his text had been printed
off, and all that he really discovered was the superiority of
the MS. to the printed texts. His ignorance of the language of the poem, even after very careful study of it, is
frequently surprising, but his remarks are often acute, and
he certainly made a most gallant attempt to better the text
in the face of great difficulties. In his Introduction to the
second edition (1823), p. ix, he has this remarkable utterance: " Whoever, therefore, shall hereafter aspire to the
honour of editing the King's Quair, will neither satisfy his
own wishes nor the public expectation, unless he brings to
the task a mind prepared by habits of strict analysis, by a
mature acquaintance with the English writers of the fourteenth century, by considerable experience in decyphering
ancient manuscripts, and a thorough (personal) collation
of the Seldenian Quair," i.e. with the MS. This is just;
and this is why I first of all put aside all previous editions,
and started afresh with a transcript from the Selden MS.,
and a subsequent collation of the proof-sheets with the MS.
itself, so as to make sure of every letter and every stroke.
The result was, as I expected, that the MS. has not had
justice done to it; the large number of small inaccuracies
in the old editions has caused many needless difficulties,
which are now cleared up; and it is at last possible to consult all the notes and comments given in the editions without being misled by them, which is a material point. I will

only add, that the very common practice of reprinting old printed texts, without consulting the MSS. from which those texts were printed, is most reprehensible, as it often ensures the needless perpetuation of the strangest blunders. It is the more unsafe, because many examples are known in which editors had no familiarity either with MSS. or with the grammar of the language which they professed to interpret; but the story of their incompetency is a melancholy one, nor is this the place for discussing it.

§ 22. The unique MS. of the Kingis Quair is in the Bodleian Library at Oxford, where it is marked "Arch. Selden, B. 24." It is a MS. on paper, containing numerous poems and treatises, and, in particular, some poems by Chaucer. The Kingis Quair begins on leaf 192, and ends on leaf 211. It is not all in one handwriting; the hand changes at st. 178, the latter part of the poem being in a somewhat smaller handwriting. There is also a slight change here in the system of spelling, but it is not sufficient to be worth a detailed discussion. On leaf 120 of the MS. the date 1472 occurs; and the date of the MS. itself is about 1475, or half a century after the date of composition of the poem. I take it to be a somewhat faulty transcript from a fairly good original. Most of the mistakes arise from the occasional omission of words or syllables. In st. 160, l. 4, the scribe had a couple of words before him which he could not read; so he left them out. In st. 47, he repeats the last word of l. 4 at the end of l. 5. The various footnotes point out most of the scribe's errors. It is pleasant to see how some of the old misconceptions are cleared away. I will cite just one example by way of specimen. In st. 24, l. 2, we have: "So infortunate was vs that fremyt day." This means, "That strange (or adverse) day was so unfortunate for us"; and *vs*

is here the dative case, just as *thee* is the dative case in the
expression, "O well is *thee*, and happy mayst thou be."
But Tytler misprinted *we* for *vs*, and was duly followed by
Sibbald and E. Thomson. Chalmers, indeed, alters the
phrase to *were we*, thus succeeding in getting *two* words
wrong instead of *one!* But what are we to think of editors
who were contented to leave such a glaring false concord[1]
as *we was* without a word of comment?

§ 23. As the unique MS. is thus our only guide, I decided
to exhibit it with the closest possible accuracy; and for this
purpose I have adopted the method which has been found
so satisfactory by the Early English Text Society—viz.,
that of exhibiting every mark of abbreviation and contraction in the MS. by the use of italic letters.[2] These italics
practically tell us that certain letters are not fully expressed,
but only indicated by various signs and marks. The value
of the method consists in this, that it is a guarantee to the
reader that the editor has done his work carefully. It is
even more than this; for the reader who is himself skilled
in deciphering MSS. knows at once what form these marks
of contraction would take, and is thus put in as good a position as if he had the MS. itself before him. If the editor
has made a mistake, he can correct it; and, in fact, I have
more than once rightly corrected a misread word in texts
thus carefully represented, whereas in a manipulated text
the chance of doing this is often taken away. The printing
of *v* for *u*, and of *j* for *I*, so extremely common, is a great
mistake, and leads to errors which cannot easily be seen
through. An objection has been raised, that the use of
italic letters offends the eye. The answer to this is, that

---

[1] It was such in the *old* language.

[2] A misunderstanding as to the value of my carefully prepared transcript led
to much delay.

the eye soon becomes accustomed to it, and the gain in accuracy is worth much ; whilst the attempt to make things pleasant by the alteration of MS. forms to suit modern ideas leads, in practice, to numerous inaccuracies. The editor is then no longer fully responsible, and knows that if he makes a mistake he is not likely to be found out. If it be a fact, as it is, that the word *us* was commonly written *vs*, or again, that *v* between two vowels was written *u*, why are such facts to be carefully suppressed?[1] If we exhibit the old spelling at all, let us represent it just as it really was.

§ 24. For those who are not experienced in the use of marks of abbreviation by the old scribes, I proceed to explain them fully.

(*a*) A well-defined upward curl at the end of a word or syllable signifies *er*. Examples occur in diue*r*se (2), bett*er* (2), eu*er* (5), recou*er* (5), &c. This abbreviation is extremely common.

(*b*) But if this curl occur after *p*, it then means *re*, as in p*re*sence (miswritten p*re*sene by a mere slip), in st. 166. This is because there is another symbol for p*er*, which is represented by drawing a horizontal stroke through the tail of the *p*, as in prop*er*ly (3).

(*c*) A curl like an ill-shaped *v*, but much .extended horizontally, stands for *vr* or *ur*. It occurs in p*ur*pose (5), tu*r*nyt (6), tu*r*ment (19), &c.

(*d*) A curl, first upward, then crossed, and finally brought downwards, represents *es* or *is ;* in Northern MSS. it may be taken to mean *is*. It occurs in spek*is* (12), rokk*is* (17), bok*is* (19), schour*is* (20), flour*is* (21), &c.

What happens is this : a MS. has a word which may be read as *lene* or as *leue*. The editor reads it as *leue*, but prints it *leve*. If it be wrong, how is the unwary reader to detect the error ?

(*e*) A curl very closely resembling the figure 9 means *us*. It occurs in Synthi*us* (20), th*us* (27, 69), ven*us* (52, 150), &c.

(*f*) A small undotted *i* above the line means *ri*. Examples are: enp*ri*se (20), p*ri*sou*n* (25), p*ri*ncesse (43), p*ri*uely (89).

(*g*) A stroke above a vowel, especially at the end of a word, means *m* or *n*; when over *ou*, it means *n*. Examples of *m* are few, but we find cu*m*myth (36), cu*m*myn (40), wo*m*manly (50), cu*m*myng (126), bla*m*e (195). Examples of *n* are very common, as in aue*n*ture (10), ma*n* (11), my*n* (12), resou*n* (7), p*ri*sou*n* (25), orisou*n* (53), &c. But it is frequently the case that this stroke is superfluously added when a word already contains *m* or *n*; and then there is no way of representing it except by printing it as written. Hence the forms form̄ (46), tham̄ (115), matyñs (11), anoñ (40), douñ (8), souñ (13). It is also superfluous in sleūth (186), ʒoūth (193). Difficult words of this class are hu*m*ily (106, 176), which Tytler and the rest misprint *truely*, to which it bears no resemblance; and mīster, *i.e.* mi*n*ster, or rather mi*n*ister (43), which Tytler prints as *mester*, though it makes no sense, the proper sense of *mester* being 'a trade.'

(*h*) A small *t* above the line stands for *ght* or *cht*. As *gh* (not *ch*) is occasionally written in the MS., we must take it to be *ght*. Examples: no*ght* (2), my*ght* (2), tho*ght* (5, 12), &c.

(*i*) A very difficult and doubtful sign is a very slight curl at the end of a word. It frequently means final *e*, but is sometimes meaningless. Examples are: efter*e* (3), their*e* (6), mater*e* (8), ver*e* (20). In some cases, the final *e* is essential, as it constitutes an additional syllable. Examples: fair*e* (7), four*e* (21).

(*k*) Another difficult symbol is a long *s* followed by a

downward crooked stroke; it closely resembles the German ß. This seems best expressed by *se*, as in wis*e* (12), deuis*e* (12), cas*e* (16), arys*e* (20), &c. It is sometimes preceded by a second *s*, as in distress*e* (5, 10), doubilness*e* (18), process*e* (19). The difficulty is, that in some instances it certainly means *sis*, as in cours*is* (108); but this usage is mostly confined to plural substantives.

(*l*) Some words are systematically abbreviated. Thus y^t stands for þ^t, to be printed as þ*at* or th*at*, as in stanzas 3, 6, 8, 9, 10, 11, &c. So also y^e for þe or the; I print it 'the' (187, 197). Also w^t for w*ith* (13, 19, 23, 24, &c.). Also q^d for q*uod* (139, 142, 169, 172). The symbol & for *and* is very common, but as there is no doubt about it, I print it simply 'and'; it occurs in st. 23, 33, 35, 71, &c. Other abbreviated words are tho*u* (195), ȝo*ur* (34, 43, 52, 63), ȝo*u* (34, 73, 141), thro*u* (41). The word 'present' is commonly written pn̄t, to be read as p*resent* (106). Tytler, not understanding this, prints 'pent,' which others follow. The prefix *com* is denoted in MSS. by a symbol closely resembling a 'q'; hence Tytler actually prints 'qmune' (147, 149), and 'qmonly' (119), and others follow him! The indefinite article *a* is occasionally joined to the word following it, as in alyte (49), written a lyte (53). The letter *j* is denoted by (capital) I, as in Iangill (38), Ionettis (47), pape-Iay (110). But the same symbol often means *i*, as in Infortune (5), Incidence (7). The letter ȝ occurs frequently, and is best represented by a special symbol. In the present poem, it is only used for the sound of *y* initially, but it is not uncommon for *gh* in words such as *liȝt* for *light*, and the like; and it is because its use is indeterminate that it is best to retain it. It occurs in ȝouth (9), ȝe (11), ȝeris (22), and the like; put for youth, ye, yeris.

(*m*) Other peculiarities, common to nearly all MSS., are the use of capital letters where we do not now write them, as in In (27); and the use of small letters where we now write capitals, as in god (44). The letter *u*, between two vowels, is to be sounded as *v*, as in diuerse (2), pouert (3); whilst initial *v* sometimes stands for *u*, as in vp (9), vs (24).

The parts of compound words are frequently separated; in such cases, I unite them by a hyphen, as in for-walowit (11), written as two words in the MS. Lastly, in order to assist the reader in scanning the lines, I have marked the final or medial *e*, where it constitutes a syllable, with a mark of diæresis, as in the case of thilkë (5), sterëles (15). Words or letters not found in the MS., but supplied by myself, are enclosed within square brackets, as in st. 8, l. 1, st. 16, l. 3. Tytler freely supplies words out of his own head *without any such hint*. Thus he prints the last line of st. 107 after the following fashion :—

"That langis not to me to writh, God allone."

"Will it be believed" (exclaims Mr E. Thomson) "that the word *God* is not in [the] MS.?" The strangest part of the matter is that the line, when thus manipulated, is the most hopeless nonsense. But readers in general have very little notion how often they have been mystified by editors, especially in the "good old times." Lastly, it may be remarked that the MS. is, as usual, wholly without marks of punctuation. Every editor punctuates as seems best in his own eyes; and I have restored sense in a great many places by the mere shifting of a comma. The general spelling of the scribe is good, being to a great extent phonetic, though the pronunciation of those days was different from that now in vogue. The scribe's worst mistake is the very common one of putting a final *e* at the end of a word where it is perfectly useless and otiose, as in *fruyte* (7), *frende* (10), *oure-hayle* (10), *sodaynlye* (11), *wayke* (14), and the like. And he often omits the same letter, where he should not have done so, as has been said. In many places, the final *e* (in the Northern dialect) merely denotes, as in modern English, that the *preceding* vowel is long ; as in *tyme* (5), *sone* (11).

§ 25. The general result is such as might have been expected. With all the scribe's errors, *his* copy of the poem, when accurately reproduced, is, for the most part, extremely easy to understand, and leaves us in a state of wonderment as to the singular mode of procedure hitherto adopted. The " ingenious young gentleman " on whom the world has hitherto depended doubtless did the best he could, and it is to his credit that he copied the MS. for the public benefit. But he does not seem to have been always able to read the scribe's handwriting, and he thus introduced numerous needless difficulties, which the editors in some instances attempted to remove by guesswork, whilst in other cases they have allowed the most glaring nonsense to stand in the text, without a word of remark as to the impossibility of understanding it. For instances of this, see the description of Tytler's edition just below.

§ 26. It remains to give some account of the various printed editions. Perhaps the following list is not exhaustive, but it at any rate mentions the editions which are of most importance.

A. In 1783, a century ago, appeared anonymously the " Poetical Remains of James the First, King of Scotland ; Edinburgh, printed for J. and E. Balfour, 1783." It contains a Dissertation on the Life and Writings of King James I., Remarks on Christ's Kirk of the Green, and on the King's

Quair; the texts of these poems; and a Dissertation on the Scottish Music. The editor was William Tytler, Esq., Writer to the Signet, and father of Lord Woodhouselee. A copy of the work here described, in the British Museum, contains also a short account of him, cut out of the European Magazine. He tells us that the King's Quair "was never before published." The editor's attention was drawn to it by a notice by Bishop Tanner, who had observed it amongst the Selden MSS. in the Bodleian Library. After an unsuccessful search for the MS., he at last applied "to an ingenious young gentleman, a student of Oxford, who undertook the task, and found the MS. accordingly. From a very accurate copy made by him" (says Mr Tytler) "the present publication is given." Unfortunately, the transcript was by no means a good one; and the following examples of misreadings and misapprehensions exhibit extraordinary nonsense :—

(a) "And freschly in thair birdis kynd araid,
      Thaire fatheris new, and fret thame in the sonne" (35).

To make sense, delete the comma after *araid*, and read *fetheris*, as in the MS.

(b)   "So fere forth of my lyf the hevy lyne,
           Without confort in sorowe, abandoune
           The second sistere, lukit hath to tuyne,
           Nere, by the space of zeris twice nyne," &c. (25).

To make sense, alter the punctuation.

(c)   "To lyve under zour law and so seruise" (52).

For *so* read *do*, as in the MS.

(d)   "And, quhen sche walkit, had a lytill thrawe " (67)

Delete both the commas.

(e)   "There saw I sitt in order by thame *one*
           With *hedis hore*," &c. (80).

Here the words in italics are so printed, and in other places
we find words printed in italics for no discoverable reason.
Tytler clearly supposed the above sentence to mean "*one*
with *hoary head*," for he explains it by "*Prudence*, with his
hoary head." But *hedis* is plural. For the true sense, see
the note, p. 76.

(*f*)   "And othir moyt I cannot on avise" (97).

For *moyt* the MS. has *mo y'*, i.e. (others) besides, that.

(*g*)   "O anker and treue, of oure gude aventure" (100).

For *treue* read *keye*, and delete the comma ; see the note.
Other examples might be added ; thus in st. 4, the word
poetly is printed ɸoetly ; see the note. In stanza 24, *was
vs* is printed *was we*, in defiance of grammar. In st. 36, *men*
is printed *one*. In st. 45, *I-fallyn* (pp.) is printed *I fallying*.
In st. 46, *emeraut* is printed *emerant*. In st. 106, *present* is
printed *pent ;* and, only two lines above, *humily* is printed
truely. In st. 135, *fatoure* becomes *satoure*, which Chalmers
explains by satyr ! In st. 178, *list* is printed *lefe*. In st. 185,
lufe is printed *lyfe ;* see the note. In st. 193, *ʒok* is printed
rok ; one wonders how "the rock of love" can be said to be
"easy and sure." The queerest thing of all is the printing
of an italic *Q* upside down, thus ☌, where the MS. merely
has *&*, as usual ; and the equally queer explanation that
this singular symbol stands for the word *askewis* [pre-
sumably *as Q is*] ; see note to st. 160. I draw attention to
these points because it is easy to test the later editions by
seeing how they are there treated. Nevertheless, with all
its faults, Tytler's edition is certainly, upon the whole, the
best. He took a good deal of trouble about the matter,
and wrote numerous notes upon the poem, many of which
are either interesting or helpful ; and later editors have not

been slow to avail themselves of the information which they contain. They must, however, be consulted with caution, as he occasionally wholly mistakes the language of the author. Thus, in st. 44, the phrase *that dooth me sike* means "that causes me to sigh"; but Tytler's note is, "The word *site*, or *syte*, in our old language, signifies grief or sorrow," which has nothing to do with the question. Again, in st. 53, Tytler rightly prints the last word as *plyte, i.e.* plight; but in his note he alters it to *pleyte*, remarking that "*pleyt* (sic), according to Chaucer, is a wreath or collar." In st. 56, he supposes *deuil, i.e.* devil, to be "the French *deuil*, sorrow"; and gives a false interpretation of the line accordingly. In st. 110, the transcriber wrote *tavartis* for *tabardis*, but Tytler guessed what was meant. He was not so fortunate in st. 116, where the transcriber wrote *yvete* for *ybete*, but explains *yvete* as "*y-wet* with my tears." It is also necessary to observe that the description of the Lady Joan cannot have been borrowed, as he supposes, from "Chaucer's Court of Love," for the reason that the poem so called is not Chaucer's, and is written in a form of English later than the former half of the fifteenth century.

B. "The works of James I., King of Scotland, containing the King's Quhair, Christis Kirk of the Grene, and Peblis to the Play. Perth, 1786." This is an anonymous edition; the editor's name was Robert Morison. It is practically a mere reprint of Tytler. The notes are "extracted (by permission)" from Tytler's. They are much abbreviated, and occupy only six pages. The volume also contains "Two ancient Scotish poems, commonly ascribed to King James V." These are (1) The Gaberlunzie Man; and (2) A Ballad of the Jollie Beggar, of which it is remarked that it "is surely *not* the composition of King James." It contains one correction of Tytler's text—viz., in st. 161, where it is said that "the MS. has *Degoutit*, from the French word, *i.e.* spotted." This is right; Tytler has the unmeaning form *Degontit.*

C. In Sibbald's Chronicle of Scottish Poetry, 4 vols., Edinburgh, 1802, a large portion of the Kingis Quair is printed at pp. 14-54 of vol. i. He includes the whole of the poem excepting st. 1-19, 116-120, 182-186, 188-193, 195, 196; thus printing 160 stanzas out of 197. He numbers his stanzas from 1 to 160 continuously, so that his numbering does not agree with that of any other edition, nor does it show which are the omitted stanzas. He tells us that "this is the first *corrected* copy"; but the claim is not to be allowed. He attains, indeed, to the right reading *list* for Tytler's *lefe* in st. 178, l. 4; he proposes to read "To *pere* with perll," *i.e.* to be a peer to pearl, in the last line of st. 110, which is a great improvement; and he alters Tytler's *satoure* in st. 135 to *feator*, which is nearer to the MS. spelling *fatoure*. But it is evident that all he did was to send *a copy of Tytler's book* to the press, since the peculiarities of the first edition in printing certain words (needlessly and for no apparent reason) in italics, are all reproduced, as well as the very strange colophon beginning "EXPLICIT, ZIC, ZIC"; where ZIC is Tytler's singular way of printing &c. Indeed, he not only gives us again most of Tytler's errors, such as *we* for *vs* (24), *fatheris* for *fetheris* (35), *mester* for *minister* (43), *pent* for *present* (106), *tavartis* (110), *fund in* for *fundin* (169); but he introduces fresh errors of his own, such as *cost* for *cast* (60); *bruckt* (which is nonsense) for *gruch* (91); *trige* (which is nonsense) for Tytler's *treue*, the MS. reading being *keye* (100); *flouris* for *floure* (187); *impunis* for *impnis* (197). It will be seen, therefore, that his "corrected copy" is of less value than the copy which he corrects.

D. The fourth edition is that of E. Thomson in 1815; see description of *F.* below, p. l.

E. I next notice "The Poetic Remains of some of The Scotish Kings, now first collected by George Chalmers, Esq., F.R.S.A.S., &c., London, 1824." I take this edition to be much the worst of all; and its worthlessness is aggravated by the author's peculiarly dishonest course of procedure. He first quotes from Pinkerton's Scotish Poems, 1792, p. xxxvi, a statement that Tytler's text had been collated with the MS., when it was said to exhibit "upwards of three hundred variations, most of which are essential to the sense" (a statement which is certainly exaggerated). He next tells us that "another attempt was made, at an after period, by Mr David Laing, of Edinburgh, to collate the same poem; but he desisted, without accomplishing his object, seeing, perhaps, the said *three hundred variations*" (the italics are his). Thirdly, he tells us how he requested the late Rev. Rogers Ruding to collate the MS. for him; and "he did this accordingly, and found the printed copy to have many faults." And having thus prepared us for expecting great improvements, he suddenly explains his own method of editing in the following words: "As it is thus impossible to establish anything like uniformity in the spelling of the King's Quair, it has been thought fit to adopt altogether the present practice of orthography;" in other words, he proposes to use the modern spelling throughout. But when we open the book, we find that he has done nothing of the kind! He actually prints the poem according to the worst possible method, in a *mixed* spelling. Most of the words are in modernised spelling, but the harder words are left in the old spelling, and are printed in italics. It is quite clear how this was accomplished. Having sufficiently abused Tytler's edition to throw his readers off the scent, he *sent a copy of Tytler's edition to press, in which he doubtless underlined all the hard words.* Consequently the printers printed all these words in italics, and modernised the spelling of all the rest. That this was the course adopted, becomes still clearer when we examine the footnotes to Chalmers's text; *for almost all these footnotes are exactly reprinted from the footnotes in Tytler's edition.* The matter is made still worse by the wily device of inserting "Tytler" at the end of a note on p. 52, thus naturally leading the innocent reader to suppose that the notes which are *not* so marked were written by himself. It is a comfort to think that he was found out; for Mr Irving, in his History of Scotish Poetry, ed. 1861, p. 135, speaks of Chalmers's edition in the following terms: "According to the modern practice of book-making, his [Tytler's] notes are here appropriated without the slightest acknowledgment; and the process of modernizing the spelling is in many instances equivalent to a translation." Still, not even Mr Irving seems to have discovered the ingenious process by which Mr Chalmers contrived to steal, not only without acknowledgment, but by the very help of abuse, the *text as well as the notes* of the editor who preceded him. It is true that Mr Chalmers added just a few notes of his own; but they are all of the most meagre kind, only three or four words long, and of no value; the curious reader may find them on pp. 68, 69 (note 5), 70 (note 8), 73 (note 6), 77 (note 3), 83 (note 2), 103 (note 1). I doubt if there are more which are wholly his, though in other places he adds just a few words. As a specimen, take note 6 on p. 73—

d

"*Stound*, or moment, or instant." Tytler's notes, on the other hand, are frequently of great length; one of them (Chalmers, p. 45) contains a quotation from the Court of Love, 49 lines long; another (Chalmers, p. 33) contains three quotations from Rymer's Fœdera, and various historical remarks. Moreover, after insisting on the "three hundred variations," and telling us how Mr Ruding made a collation for him, it is startling to find that he scarcely paid any attention to Mr Ruding's notes, and only made a few *silent* alterations, besides offering in the notes the six following remarks, which are all of the most trivial kind :—

St. 36, l. 7. The MS. has 'me'; Ruding. [No; 'me*n.*']

45, l. 4. The MS. has 'frre'; Ruding. [I read it 'ferr*e.*']

108, l. 7. The word 'graice' is marked for deletion, and the mark is afterwards crossed out. [I say this in a note.]

109, l. 7. The words 'foule or' are written above 'doken'; Ruding. [I read them as 'foule on.']

125, l. 5. *Sad renewe* (Chalmers). The reading is correct (Ruding). [It really means that the reading *said renewe* (Tytler) is correct, and that Chalmers altered it!]

134, l. 7. Ruding speaks of the word *hend* [I read it *heid*, but say it is obscure] as belonging here.

This is all the merest trifling. None of these notes, except the fifth, gives us any help; and there *are only a few instances throughout the whole poem* of correction of the supposed "three hundred" errors. Further comment is needless.

F. "The King's Quair, a poem, by James, King of Scots; collated with an original manuscript, and illustrated from authentic sources, &c. By Ebenezer Thomson, of Ayr Academy. Second Edition, Ayr; 1824." This is a second edition of a work, the first edition of which I have not seen, though there is a copy in the British Museum, printed at the same place in 1815. It is evident that Mr Thomson took very great pains with his work, and was extremely interested in it ; we can only regret the difficulties in which he was placed concerning it. It was not till August 1823, when the proof-sheets of the greater part of the second edition were already printed, that he at last obtained his long-cherished desire of seeing the manuscript. He at once detected most of the more important errors, and took the opportunity of recording them either in his notes, or in a list of Errata at p. 97. I cannot but sympathise with his desire to do justice to the text, and it is a pity that he was able to do so little. His text is little better than a reprint of Tytler, but there are several remarks in the notes which I have found well worth consulting. It is much to be regretted that so zealous a worker had but slight oppor- tunities, and that his book is disfigured by many remarks which reveal a sad ignorance of all philological principles. Thus he considers *tolter* as "a participle of *welter*" ; and he derives *drest* from the "Ger. *driessen*, to vex." But he had consulted Chaucer's works with diligence, and discovered that the mysterious word *deuil*, which to Tytler seemed to be the French *deuil*, mourning, was nothing but the old spelling of *devil ;* and he points to the fact that the phrase *a twenty deuil way* occurs in the Legend of Ariadne, which is one of the stories in the Legend of Good Women. He might have added that it occurs again in other passages ; see my notes to st. 56. He corrects Tytler's explanations of *dooth me sike* (44) and *pace* (69) ; and he corrects several false readings. I have carefully read his notes, and have adopted some of his illustrations.

G. An anonymous edition was printed at Glasgow in 1825. This is a mere reprint of Tytler, as is expressly stated. "The King's Quair was edited by W. Tytler, at Edinburgh, in 1783. In this new edition the editors have scrupulously followed the original printed one mentioned above." The reprint includes Tytler's Dissertation on the Scottish Music, and some Remarks on the Scottish Language; as well as a version of Peblis to the Play (p. 195), which is not included in Tytler's book, and a version of Christ's Kirk of the Greene (p. 213), which Tytler edited with the King's Quair. For the reader who desires to see Tytler's edition, and is unable to obtain it, this Glasgow reprint is almost as good as the old edition.

H. In "Specimens of English Literature from 1394 to 1579," edited by me in 1871, I gave a small portion of The Kingis Quair—viz., st. 152-173, numbered as in the present edition. I mention the fact, because this portion was edited *directly from the MS.*, and necessarily agrees throughout with that portion of the poem as it appears in the present volume. The only variation is in the use of italic *th* to represent the *y*, or rather the ill-written þ, of the MS.; in the present volume, it seemed to me sufficient to leave the "th" in roman letters, as there is no instance where the use of it leads to doubt. In the edition next mentioned, my work was ignored.

I. "The Poetical Remains of King James the First of Scotland, with a Memoir, &c. By the Rev. C. Rogers, LL.D., F.S.A. Scot., Historiographer to the Royal Historical Society. Edinburgh: printed for the Editor. 1873." This edition was limited to 150 copies only. There is a copy in the Bodleian Library, Oxford. "In the present work," says the editor, "the versions of Chalmers and Tytler have been collated, so as to form a text suitable to the period." The account of Chalmers's text above will show the want of wisdom of the plan adopted. The result is of course unsatisfactory; and if ever this volume becomes valuable, it will be solely owing to its scarcity. We find the old errors reproduced, such as *tavartis* for *tabartis*, *yvete* for *ybete*, *satoure* for *fatoure*, and the like; besides additional errors, such as *husing* for *hufing*, in st. 159, where Tytler is correct. The notes are few, and carefully avoid all difficult passages.

K. "The King's Quair; a Poem by James the First, King of Scots. John Thomson: Glasgow. 1877." This is a reprint of E. Thomson's Ayr edition of 1824; but it admits into the text the corrections made by that editor in his notes. "Beyond the endeavour to present the poem in its *corrected* form, with the best procurable notes elucidatory of its meaning, nothing has been attempted."

§ 27. It thus appears that none of the editors except E. Thomson and myself ever saw the MS., and that, for all practical purposes, they have done little beyond reprinting the first incorrect text over and over again. The only complete text that gives us anything better is the latest impression, in 1877, of E. Thomson's edition; and even this is imperfect, owing to the slight opportunity afforded him: he was only able to take some notes, "upon a rapid inspection of the MS." And hence it has come to pass that it has taken a whole century, and a series of about ten editions, merely to obtain a correct copy of a MS. which is in so accessible a place as the Bodleian Library, and does not extend to so much as fourteen hundred lines. But a great change for the better has taken place of late years in the manner of editing texts, and it is now an acknowledged principle that an accurate representation of the MS. authorities is of primary importance.

§ 28. The Notes are, to a large extent, original, though I have occasionally borrowed from Tytler and E. Thomson where they are clearly right. I also discuss some of the more remarkable variations from the MS. in the different . editions. Much gain has resulted from the comparison of the language of the poem with the language of Chaucer. We are thus able to trace a large number of parallel passages, and to establish the laws of metre (and to some extent of grammar) which guided the royal author in his work. I have also found a familiarity with the language of Barbour of much service; so that the only passages still left obscure are two or three which are manifestly corrupt, where we are left at the mercy of the scribe of the unique MS. original. With these exceptions, the language of the author is extremely simple and easy to any one who has some knowledge of Middle English; his metre is harmonious, and subject (with well-defined exceptions) to the laws which have been laid down for the scansion of Chaucer; whilst a complete scheme of his grammar might easily be deduced, and has, in a great measure, been indicated.

§ 29. The Glossarial Index is almost wholly new, and has purposely been made a very full one, with references to the stanzas. In preparing it, I have received some assistance from my eldest daughter. The only previous glossary is one three pages long, at the end of E. Thomson's edition; but it is useless from its omission of references. Some of the words are explained in Jamieson's Dictionary; and I have therefore taken the opportunity of pointing out cases' where Jamieson has been misled by Tytler, as, *e.g.*, in the case of the non-existent word *foringit*. See p. 113. Those who are interested in grammatical details will of course consult Dr Murray's essay on The Dialect of the Southern Counties of Scotland, published by Asher & Co. in 1873.

§ 30. The literary merit of the poem has been often discussed, and I have nothing more to say about it here. To point out the beauties or the demerits of a poem is not always a kindness to the reader ; for it deprives him of the pleasure of forming his own judgment upon a subject which he may be peculiarly competent to consider.

THE KINGIS QUAIR

Heirefter followis the quair Maid be King Iames of scotland the first callit the kingis quair and Maid
  quhen his Maiestie Wes In Ingland.

1 HEIGH In the hevynnis figure circulere
       The rody sterres twynklyng as the fyre;
   And, In Aquary, Citherea[1] the clere
       Rynsid hir tressis like the goldin wyre,
       That late tofore, In fair and fresche atyre,
   Through capricorn heved hir hornis bright,
   North northward approchit the myd-nyght;

2 Quhen as I lay In bed allone waking,
       New partit out of slepe a lyte tofore,
   Fell me to mynd of many diuerse thing,
       Off this and that; can I noght say quharfore,
       Bot slepe for craft in erth myght I no more;
   For quhich as tho coude I no better wyle,
   Bot toke a boke to rede apon a quhile:

3 Off quhich the name Is clepit properly
       Boece, eftere him that was the compiloure,
   Schewing [the] counsele of philosophye,
       Compilit by that noble senatoure
       Off rome, quhilom that was the warldis floure,
   And from estatë by fortune a quhile
   Foriugit was to pouert in exile:

4 And there to here this worthy lord and clerk,
       His metir suete, full of moralitee;
   His flourit pen so fair he set a-werk,

                    [1] *Read* Cinthia.

Discryving first of his prosperitee,
And out of that his infelicitee;
And than how he, in his poetly report,
In philosophy can him to confort.

5 For quhich thoght I in purpose, at my boke,
To borowe a slepe at thilkē tyme began;
Or euer I stent, my best was more to loke
Vpon the writing of this noble man,
That in him-self the full recouer wan
Off his Infortune, pouert,[1] and distresse,
And in tham set his verray sekernesse.

6 And so the vertew of his ȝouth before
Was in his age the ground of his delytis:
Fortune the bak him turnyt, and therfore
He makith Ioye and confort, that he quit is[2]
Off theire[3] vnsekir warldis appetitis;
And so aworth he takith his penance,
And of his vertew maid It suffisance:

7 With mony a noble resoun, as him likit,
Enditing In his faire latyne tong,
So full of fruyte, and rethorikly pykit,
Quhich to declare my scole is ouer ȝong;
Therefore I lat him pas, and, in my tong,
Procede I will agayn to my sentence
Off my mater, and leue all Incidence.

8 The long[ë] nyght beholding, as I saide,
Myn eyën[4] gan to smert for studying;
My buke I schet, and at my hede It laide;
And douñ I lay bot ony tarying,
This matere new[ë] In my mynd rolling;

---

[1] MS. pouerti; *but the* i *is ignorantly added by a later hand.*
[2] MS. quitis.   [3] *Read* thir.   [4] MS. eyne; *see* st. 41.

This Is to seynë, how th*a*t eche estate,
As fortune lykith, thame will [oft] translate.

9 For sothe It is, th*a*t, on hir tolt*er* quhele,
    Eu*er*y wight cleu*er*ith In his stage,
And failyng foting oft, quhen hir lest rele,
    Sum vp, sum douñ, Is noñ estate nor age
    Ensured, more the pryncë than the page :
So vncouthly hir werdes sche deuidith,
Namly In ʒouth, that seildin ought prouidith.

10 Among thir thoughtis rolling to and fro,
    Fell me to mynd of my fortune and vre ;
In tend*er* ʒouth how sche was first my fo,
    And eft my frende, and how I gat recure
    Off my distress*e*, and all my*n* aue*n*ture
I gan our*e*-hayle, that lang*er* slepe ne rest
Ne myg*h*t I nat, so were my wittis wrest.

11 For-wakit and for-walowit, thus musing,
    Wery, forlyin, I lestnyt sodaynlye,
And sone I herd the bell to matyñs ryng,
    And vp I ras*e*, no lang*er* wald I lye :
    Bot now, how trowe ʒe ? suich a fantasye
Fell me to mynd, that ay me thog*h*t the bell
Said to me, " tell on, ma*n*, quhat the befell."

12 Thog*h*t I tho to my-self, " quhat may this be ?
    This is my*n* awin ymagynaciou*n* ;
It is no lyf that spek*is* vnto me ;
    It is a bell, or that impressiou*n*
    Off my thog*h*t causith this Illusiou*n*,
That dooth me think so nycely i*n* this wis*e* ; "
And so befell as I schall ʒou deuis*e*.

13 Determyt furth there*with* In myn entent,
    Sen I thus haue ymagynit of this souñ,
And in my tyme more Ink and pap*er* spent
    To lyte effect, I tuke conclusiou*n*
    Sum new[ë] thing to write ; I set me douñ,
And furth-w*ith*-all my pen In hand I tuke,
And maid a ✠, and thus begouth my buke.

14 THOU [sely]¹ ȝouth, of nature Indegest,
    Vnrypit fruyte w*ith* windis variable ;
Like to the bird th*at* fed is on the nest,
    And can no*ght* flee ; of wit wayke and vnstable,
    To fortune both and to Infortune hable ;
Wist thou thy payne to cum² and thy trauaille,
For sorow and drede wele my*ght* thou wepe and waille.

15 Thus stant thy confort In vnseke*r*nesse*e*,
    And wantis It th*at* suld the reule and gye :
Ry*ght* as the schip th*at* sailith sterëles
    Vpon the rok[kis]³ most to harmes hye,
    For lak of It th*at* suld bene hir supplye ;
So standis thou here In this warldis rage,
And wantis th*at* suld gyde all thy viage.

16 I mene this by my-self, as In partye ;
    Though nature gave me suffisance In ȝouth,
The rypeness*e* of resou*n* [ȝit] lak[it] I,
    To gouerne with my will ; so lyte I couth,
    Quhen sterëles to trauaile I begouth,
Amang the wawis of this warld to driue ;
And how the cas*e*, anoñ I will discriue.

¹ MS. Though (*for* Thou) ; sely *is omitted* ; cf. st. 44, 134.
² MS. tocum (*one word*).
³ MS. rok ; *but see* st. 17, l. 1 ; st. 18, l. 1.

17 With doutfull hert, amang the rokk*is* blake,
　　My feble bote full fast to stere and rowe,
Helples allone, the wynt*er* nyg*h*t I wake,
　　　To wayte the wynd th*a*t furthward suld me throwe.
　　　O empti saile ! quhare is the wynd suld blowe
Me to the port, quhar gy*n*neth all my game?
Help, Calyope, and wynd, in Marye name !

18 The rokkis clepe I the prolixitee
　　　Off doubilness*e tha*t doith my wittis pall :
The lak of wynd is the deficultee
　　　In enditing of this lytill trety small :
　　　The bote I clepe the mat*er* hole of all :
My wit vnto the saile th*a*t now I wynd,
To seke co*n*nyng, though I bot lytill fynd.

19 At my begy*n*nyng first I clepe and call
　　　To ʒow, Cleo, and to ʒow, polymye,
W*ith* Thesiphone, goddis and sistris all,
　　　In nowm*er* ix., as bok*is* specifye ;
　　　In this process*e* my wilsum wittis gye ;
And w*ith* ʒo*ur* bryg*h*t lant*er*nis wele conuoye
My pen, to write my t*ur*ment and my Ioye !

20 In ver*e*, th*a*t full of vertu is and gude,
　　　Quhen nature first begy*n*neth hir enp*r*is*e*,
That quhilum was be cruell frost and flude
　　　And schour*is* scharp opprest In many wys*e*,
　　　And Synthi*us* [be]gy*n*neth to arys*e*
Heigh in the est, a morow soft and suete,
Vpward his cours*e* to driue In ariete :

21 Passit mydday bot[1] four*e* greis evin,
　　　Off lenth and brede his angel wingis bryg*h*t
He spred vpon the ground douñ fro the hevin ;
　　　　　　　[1] MS. Passit bot mydday.

That, for gladnesse and confort[1] of the sight,
    And with the tiklyng of his hete and light,
The tender flouris opnyt thame and sprad;
    And, in thaire nature, thankit him for glad.

22 Noght fer passit the state of Innocence,
    Bot nere about the nowmer of ʒeris thre,
Were It causit throu hevinly Influence
    Off goddis will, or othir casualtee,
    Can I noght say; bot out of my contree,
By thaire avise that had of me the cure,
Be see to pas, tuke I myn auenture.

23 Puruait of all that was vs necessarye,
    With wynd at will, vp airly by the morowe,
Streight vnto schip, no longere wold we tarye,
    The way we tuke, the tyme I tald to-forowe;
    With mony "fare wele" and "sanct Iohne to borowe"
Off falowe and frende; and thus with one assent
We pullit vp saile, and furth oure wayis went.

24 Vpon the wawis weltering to and fro,
    So infortunate was vs that fremyt day,
That maugre, playnly, quhethir we wold or no,
    With strong hand, [as] by forse, schortly to say,
    Off Inymyis takin and led away
We weren all, and broght in thaire contree;
Fortune It schupe noñ othir wayis to be.

25 Quhare as In strayte ward and in strong prisoun,
    So fer-forth, of my lyf the heuy lyne,
Without confort, in sorowe abandouñ,
    The secund sistere lukit hath to twyne,
    Nere by the space of ʒeris twise[2] nyne;

---

[1] Confort, *in the margin, is substituted for* freschenesse.
[2] *Read* twiës (the usual Chaucerian dissyllabic form).

Till Iupiter his merci list aduert,
And send confort in relesche of my smert.

26 Quhare as In ward full oft I wold bewaille
   My dedely lyf, full of peyne and penance,
Saing ryght thus, quhat haue I gilt to faille
   My fredome in this warld and my plesance?
   Sen euery wight has thereof suffisance,
That I behold, and I a creature
Put from all this—hard Is myn auenture!

27 The bird, the beste, the fisch eke In the see,
   They lyve in fredome euerich In his kynd;
And I a man, and lakkith libertee;
   Quhat schall I seyne, quhat resoun may I fynd,
   That fortune suld do so? thus In my mynd
My folk I wold argewe, bot all for noght;
Was non that myght, that on my peynes rought.

28 Than wold I say, "gif god me had deuisit
   To lyve my lyf in thraldome thus and pyne,
Quhat was the cause that he [me] more comprisit
   Than othir folk to lyve in suich ruyne?
   I suffer allone amang the figuris nyne,
Ane wofull wrecche that to no wight may spede,
And ȝit of euery lyvis help[1] hath nede."

29 The long[e] dayes and the nyghtis eke
   I wold bewaille my fortune in this wise,
For quhich, agane distresse confort to seke,
   My custum was on mornis for to ryse
   Airly as day; o happy excercise!
By the come I to Ioye out of turment.
Bot now to purpose of my first entent :—

[1] In drede *was written after* help, *but is crossed through.*

30 Bewailing In my chamber thus allone,
    Despeired of all Ioye and remedye,
For-tirit of my thoght, and wo begone,
    Unto[1] the wyndow gan I walk In hye,
    To se the warld and folk that went forby;
As for the tyme, though I of mirthis fude
Myght haue no more, to luke It did me gude.

31 Now was there maid fast by the touris wall
    A gardyn faire, and in the corneris set
Ane herbere grene, with wandis long and small
    Railit about; and so with treis set
    Was all the place, and hawthorn hegis knet,
That lyf was noñ walking there forby,
That myght within scarse ony wight aspye.

32 So thik the bewis and the leues grene
    Beschadit all the aleyes that there were,
And myddis euery herbere myght be sene
    The scharp[ë] grenë suetë Ienepere,
    Growing so faire with branchis here and there,
That, as It semyt to a lyf without,
The bewis spred the herbere all about;

33 And on the small[ë] grenë twistis sat
    The lytill suetë nyghtingale, and song
So loud and clere, the ympnis consecrat
    Off lufis vse, now soft, now lowd among,
    That all the gardyng and the wallis rong
Ryght of thaire song, and on[2] the copill next
Off thaire suete armony, and lo the text:

Cantus.

34 "Worschippë, ʒe that loueris bene, this may,
    For of ʒour blisse the kalendis are begonne,
And sing with vs, away, winter, away!

[1] MS. And to.   [2] *Perhaps we should read* of.

Cum, som*er*, cum, the suete sesou*n* and sonne !
Awake for schame ! that haue ჳo*ur* hevy*n*nis wonne,
And amorously lift vp ჳo*ur* hedis all,
Thank lufe that list ჳo*u* to his merci call."

35 Quhen thai this song had song a lytill thrawe,
  Thai stent a quhile, and ther*ewith* vnaffraid,
As I beheld and kest my*n* eyne a-lawe,
  From beugh to beugh thay hippit and thai plaid,
  And freschly in thair*e* birdis kynd arraid
Thair*e* fether*is* new, and fret thame In the sonne,
And thankit lufe, that had thair*e* makis wonne.

36 This was the planë ditee of thair*e* note,
  And ther*e-with*-all vnto my-self I thog*h*t,
"Quhat lyf is this, that mak*is* bird*is* dote ?
  Quhat may this be, how cu*m*myth It of ought ?
  Quhat nedith It to be so dere ybought ?
It is nothing, trowe I, bot feynit chere,
And that me*n* list to count*er*feten chere."

37 Eſt wald I think ; "o lord, quhat may this be ?
  That lufe is of so noble myg*h*t and kynde,
Lufing his folk, and suich prosperitee
  Is It of him, as we in buk*is* fynd ?
  May he our*e* hertes setten and vnbynd ?
Hath he vpon oure hertis suich maistrye ?
Or all this is bot feynyt fantasye !

38 For gif he be of so grete excellence,
  That he of eu*er*y wight hath cure and charge,
Quhat haue I gilt to him or doon offense,
  That I am thrall, and birdis gone at large,
  Sen him to s*er*ue he myg*h*t set my corage ?

And gif he be no*gh*t so, than may I seyne,
Quhat mak*is* folk to Iangill of him In veyne?

39 Can I no*gh*t elles fynd, bot gif th*a*t he
       Be lord, and as a god may lyue and regne,
    To bynd and lous*e*, and maken thrallis free,
       Than wold I pray his blisfull grace benigne,
       To hable me vnto his s*er*uice digne ;
    And eu*er*more for to be one of tho
    Him trewly for to s*er*ue In wele and wo.

40 And there-*with* kest I douñ my*n* eye ageyne,
       Quhare as I sawe, walking vnd*er* the tour*e*,
    Full secretly new cu*m*myn hir to pleyne,
       The fairest or the freschest ʒong[ë] floure
       That eu*er* I sawe, me tho*gh*t, befor*e* that houre,
    For quhich sodayn abate, anoñ astert
    The blude of all my body to my hert.

41 And though I stude abaisit tho a lyte,
       No wond*er* was ; for-quhy my wittis all
    Were so ou*er*cọ̃m *with* plesance and delyte,
       Onely throu latting of my*n* eyën fall,
       That sudaynly my hert became hir thrall,
    For eu*er*, of free wyll ; for of manace
    There was no takyn In hir suetë face.

42 And In my hede I drewe ry*gh*t hastily,
       And eft-sonës I lent It forth ageyne,
    And sawe hir walk, that verray woma*n*ly,
       W*ith* no wight mo, bot onely wom*m*en tueyne.
       Than gan I studye in my-self and seyne,
    "A ! suete, ar ʒe a warldly creature,
    Or hevinly thing in likeness*e* of nature ?

43 Or ar ʒe god Cupidis owin princesse,
    And cummyn are to louse me out of band?
Or ar ʒe verray nature the goddesse,
    That haue depaynted with ʒour hevinly hand
    This gardyn full of flouris, as they stand?
Quhat sall I think, allace! quhat reuerence
Sall I min[i]ster to ʒour excellence?

44 Gif ʒe a goddesse be, and that ʒe like
    To do me payne, I may It noght astert;
Gif ʒe be warldly wight, that dooth me sike,
    Quhy lest god mak ʒou so, my derrest hert,
    To do a sely prisoner thus smert,
That lufis ʒow all, and wote of noght bot wo?
And therefor, merci, suete! sen It is so."

45 Quhen I a lytill thrawe had maid my moon,
    Bewailling myn infortune and my chance,
Vnknawin how or quhat was best to doon,
    So ferre I-fallyng Into lufis dance,
    That sodeynly my wit, my contenance,
My hert, my will, my nature, and my mynd,
Was changit clene ryght In añ-othir kynd.

46 Off hir array the form gif I sall write,
    Toward hir goldin haire and rich atyre
In fret-wise couchit [was] with perllis quhite
    And gretë balas lemyng as the fyre,
    With mony ane emeraut and faire saphire;
And on hir hede a chaplet fresch of hewe,
Off plumys partit rede, and quhite, and blewe;

47 Full of quaking spangis bryght as gold,
    Forgit of schap like to the amorettis,
So new, so fresch, so plesant to behold,

The plumys eke like to the floure-Ionett*is*,
    And othir of schap like to the [round crokettis],[1]
And, aboue all this, there was, wele I wote,
Beautee eneuch to mak a world to dote.

48 About hir nek, quhite as the fyre amaille,
    A gudely cheyne of smale orfeuerye,
Quhar*e*by there hang a ruby, w*it*/out faille,
    Lyke to ane hert[ë] schapin verily,
    That, as a sperk of lowe, so wantoñly
Semyt birnyng vpon hir quhytë throte ;
Now gif there was gud p*a*rtye, god It wote !

49 And forto walk that freschë mayes morowe,
    Añ huke sche had vpon hir tissew quhite,
That gudeliar*e* had nog*h*t bene sene toforowe,
    As I suppos*e*; and girt sche was a lyte ;
    Thus halflyng lous*e* for haste, to suich delyte
It was to see hir ȝouth In gudelihed*e*,
That for rudenes to speke ther*e*of I drede.

50 In hir was ȝouth, beautee, w*it*/ humble aport,
    Bountee, richess*e*, and wo*m*manly facture,
God bett*er* wote than my pen can report :
    Wis*e*dome, largess*e*, estate, and co*n*nyng sure
    In eu*er*y poynt so guydit hir mesure,
In word, in dede, in schap, in contenance,
That natur*e* myg*h*t no more hir childe auance.

51 Throw quhich anoñ I knew and vnd*er*stude
    Wele, that sche was a warldly creature ;
On quhom to rest my*n* eyë, so mich gude
    It did my wofull hert, I ȝow assure,
    That It was to me Ioye w*it*/out mesure ;

---

[1] *The* MS. *repeats* floure Ionett*is*, *evidently by mistake; my insertion*
is conjectural.

And, at the last, my luke vnto the hevin
I threwe furthwith, and said thir versis sevin :

52 "O ven*us* clere ! of goddis stellifyit !
      To quhom I ȝelde homage and sacrifise,
Fro this day forth ȝo*ur* grace be magnifyit,
      That me ressauit haue in suich [a] wise,
      To lyve vnd*er* ȝo*ur* law and do s*er*uise ;
Now help me furth, and for ȝo*ur* m*er*ci lede
My hert to rest, th*a*t deis nere for drede."

53 Quhen I w*ith* gude entent this orisou*n*
      Thus endit had, I stynt a lytill stound ;
And eft my*n* eye full pitously adoun̄
      I kest, behalding vnto hir lytill hound,
      That w*ith* his bellis playit on the ground ;
Than wold I say, and sigh ther*e-with* a lyte,
"A ! wele were him th*a*t now were In thy plyte !"

54 An̄-othir quhile the lytill nyghtingale,
      That sat apon the twiggis, wold I chide,
And say ryg*h*t thus ; "quhare ar*e* thy notis smale,
      That thou of loue has song this morowe-tyde ?
      Seis thou nog*h*t hir*e* that sittis the besyde ?
For Ven*us* sake, the blisfull goddesse clere,
Sing on agane, and mak my lady chere.

55 And eke I pray, for all the paynes grete,
      That, for the loue of proigne thy sist*er* dere,
Thou sufferit quhilom, quhen thy brestis wete
      Were with the teres of thyne eyën clere,
      All bludy ronne ; that pitee was to here
The crueltee of that vnknyg*h*tly dede,
Quhare was fro the bereft thy maidenhede,

56 Lift vp thyne hert, and sing with gude entent;
    And in thy notis suete the treson telle,
That to thy sister trewe and Innocent
    Was kythit by hir husband false and fell;
    For quhois gilt, as It is worthy wel,
Chide thir husbandis that are false, I say,
And bid thame mend, In the twenty[1] deuil way.

57 O lytill wrecch, allace! maist thou noght se
    Quho commyth 3ond? Is It now tyme to wring?
Quhat sory thoght is fallin vpon the?
    Opyn thy throte; hastow no lest to sing?
    Allace! sen thou of reson had felyng,
Now, suetë bird, say ones to me 'pepe;'
I dee for wo; me think thou gynnis slepe.

58 Hastow no mynde of lufe? quhare is thy make?
    Or artow seke, or smyt with Ielousye?
Or Is sche dede, or hath sche the forsake?
    Quhat is the cause of thy malancolye,
    That thou no more list maken melodye?
Sluggart, for schame! lo here thy goldin houre,
That worth were hale all thy lyvis laboure!

59 Gyf thou suld sing wele euer in thy lyve,
    Here is, in fay, the tyme, and eke the space:
Quhat wostow than? sum bird may cum and stryve
    In song with the, the maistry to purchace.
    Suld thou than cesse, It were grete schame, allace!
And here, to wyn gree happily for euer,
Here is the tyme to syng, or ellis neuer."

60 I thoght eke thus, gif I my handis clap,
    Or gif I cast, than will sche flee away;
And gif I hald my[2] pes, than will sche nap;

And gif I crye, sche wate nog*h*t quhat I say :
Thus, quhat is best, wate I nog*h*t be this day :
"Bot blawe wynd, blawe, and do the leuis schake,
That sum twig may wag, and mak hir to wake."

61 With that anoñ ryg*h*t [sc]he toke vp a sang,
    Quhare com*e* anoñ mo birdis and alight ;
Bot than, to here the mirth was thañ amang,
    Ou*er* that to, to see the suetë sicht
    Off hyr ymage, my spirit was so light,
Me thog*h*t I flawe for Ioye w*i*t*h*out arest,
So were my wittis boundin all to fest.

62 And to the notis of the philomene,
    Quhilk*is* sche sang, the ditee there I maid
Direct to hir*e* th*a*t was my hertis quene,
    Withoutin quhom no songis may me glade ;
    And to that sanct, [there] walking in the schade,
My bedis thus, with humble hert entere,
Deuotly [than] I said on this manere.

63 "Quhen sall ȝou*r* m*er*ci rew vpon ȝou*r* man,
    Quhois s*er*uice is ȝit vncouth vnto ȝow ?
Sen, quhen ȝe go, ther is nog*h*t ellis than :
    Bot, hert ! quhere as the body may nog*h*t throu,
    Folow thy hevin ! quho suld be glad bot thou
That suich a gyde to folow has vnd*er*take ?
Were It throu hell, the way thou nog*h*t forsake !"

64 And eft*er* this, the birdis eu*er*ichone
    Tuke vp añ othir sang full loud and clere,
And w*i*t*h* a voce said, "wele is vs begone,
    That with our*e* makis ar*e* togid*er* here ;
    We proyne and play w*i*t*h*out dout and dangere,
All clothit In a soyte full fresch and newe,
In lufis s*er*uice besy, glad, and trewe.

B

65 And ʒe, fresche may, ay mercifull to bridis,
       Now welcum be ʒe, floure of monethis all;
   For noght onely ʒour grace vpon vs bydis,
       Bot all the warld to witnes this we call,
       That strowit hath so playnly ouer all
   With new[ë] freschë suete and tender grene,
   Oure lyf, oure lust, oure gouernoure, oure quene."

66 This was thair song, as semyt me full heye,
       With full mony vncouth suete note and schill,
   And therewith-all that faire vpward hir eye
       Wold cast amang, as It was goddis will,
       Quhare I myght se, standing allane full still,
   The faire facture that nature, for maistrye,
   In hir visage wroght had full lufingly.

67 And, quhen sche walkit had a lytill thrawe
       Vnder the suetë grenë bewis bent,
   Hir faire fresche face, as quhite as ony snawe,
       Scho turnyt has, and furth hir wayis went;
       Bot tho began myn axis and turment,
   To sene hir part, and folowe I na myght;
   Me thoght the day was turnyt into nyght.

68 Than said I thus, "quhare [un]to lyve I langer?
       Wofullest wicht, and subiect vnto peyne;
   Of peyne? no: god wote, ʒa: for thay no stranger
       May wirken ony wight, I dare wele seyne.
       How may this be, that deth and lyf, bothe tueyne,
   Sall bothe atonis in a creature
   Togidder duell, and turment thus nature?

69 I may noght ellis done bot wepe and waile,
       With-In thir cald[ë] wallis thus I-lokin;
   From henn[e]sfurth my rest is my trauaile;

My dryë thrist with teris sall I slokin,
    And on my-self bene al my harmys wrokin :
Thus bute is none ; bot venus, of hir grace,
Will schape remede, or do my spirit pace.

70 As Tantalus I trauaile ay but-les,
    That euer ylikë hailith at the well
Water to draw with buket botemles,
    And may noght spede ; quhois penance is añ hell :
    So by my-self this tale I may wele telle,
For vnto hir that herith noght I pleyne ;
Thus like to him my trauaile Is In veyne."

71 So sore thus sighit I with my-self allone,
    That turnyt is my strenth In febilnesse,
My wele in wo, my frendis all in fone,
    My lyf in deth, my lyght into dirknesse,
    My hope in feer, in dout my sekirnesse ;
Sen sche is gone : and god mote hir conuoye,
That me may gyde to turment and to Ioye !

72 The long[ë] day thus gan I prye and poure,
    Till phebus endit had his bemes bryght,
And bad go farewele euery lef and floure,
    This is to say, approch[en] gan the nyght,
    And Esperus his lampis gan to light ;
Quhen in the wyndow, still as any stone,
I bade at lenth, and, kneling, maid my mone.

73 So lang till evin, for lak of myght and mynd,
    For-wepit and for-pleynit pitously,
Ourset so sorow had bothe hert and mynd,
    That to the cold[ë] stone my hede on wrye
    I laid, and lent, amaisit verily,
Half sleping and half suouñ, In suich a wise :
And quhat I met, I will 3ou now deuise.

74 Me thog*h*t that thus all sodeynly a lyg*h*t
      In at the wyndow come quhare that I lent,
   Off quhich the chamber*e*-wyndow schone full bryg*h*t,
      And all my body so It hath ou*e*rwent,
      That of my sicht the v*e*rtew hale Iblent;
   And that w*ith*-all a voce vnto me saide,
   " I bring the confort and hele, be nog*h*t affrayde."

75 And furth anoñ It passit sodeynly,
      Quher It come In, the ryg*h*t[ë] way ageyne,
   And sone, me thog*h*t, furth at the dure in hye
      I went my weye, nas nothing me ageyne ;
      And hastily, by bothe the armes tueyne,
   I was araisit vp in-to the air*e*,
   Clippit in a cloude of cristall clere and fair*e*.

76 Ascending vpward ay fro spere to spere,
      Through air*e* and water*e* and the hotë fyre,
   Till th*a*t I come vnto the circle clere
      Off Signifer*e*, quhare fair*ë*, bryg*h*t, and schire,
      The signis schone ; and In the glade empire
   Off blisfull ven*us*, [quhar] ane cryit now
   So sudaynly, almost I wist nog*h*t how.

77 Off quhich the place, quhen [as] I coñ ther*e* nye,
      Was all, me thog*h*t, of cristall stonis wrog*h*t,
   And to the port I liftit was In hye,
      Quhare sodaynly, as quho sais at a thog*h*t,
      It opnyt, and I was anon In brog*h*t
   W*ith*in a chamb*er*, largë, rowm, and fair*e* ;
   And there I fand of peple grete repair*e*.

78 This Is to seyne, th*a*t pr*e*sent in that place
      Me thog*h*t I sawe of eu*e*ry naciou*n*
   Louer*is* th*a*t endit [had] thair*e* lyfis space

In lovis seruice, mony a mylioun,
Off quhois chancis maid is mencioun
In diuerse bukis, quho thame list to se;
And therefore here thaire namys lat I be.

79 The quhois auenture and grete labouris
   Aboue thaire hedis writin there I fand;
This is to seyne, martris and confessouris,
   Ech in his stage, and his make in his hand;
   And therewith-all thir peple sawe I stand,
With mony a solemp[ni]t contenance,
After as lufe thame lykit to auance.

80 Off gude folkis, that faire In lufe befill,
   There saw I sitt In order by thame one
With hedis hore; and with thame stude gude-will
   To talk and play; and after that anon
   Besydis [1] thame and next there saw I gone
Curage, amang the fresche folkis zong,
And with thame playit full merily and song.

81 And In ane othir stage, endlong the wall,
   There saw I stand, In capis wyde and lang,
A full grete nowmer; bot thaire hudis all,
   Wist I noght quhy, atoure thair eyën hang;
   And ay to thame come repentance amang,
And maid thame chere, degysit in his wede:
And dounward efter that zit I tuke hede;

82 Ryght ouerthwert the chamber was there drawe
   A trevesse thin and quhite, all of plesance,
The quhich behynd, standing there I sawe
   A warld of folk, and by thaire contenance
   Thaire hertis semyt full of displesance,

[1] MS. Besyde (badly).

With billis In thaire handis, of one assent
Vnto the Iuge thaire playntis to present.

83 And there-with-all apperit vnto me
        A voce, and said, "tak hede, man, and behold :
    ȝonder [1] thou seis the hiest stage and gree
        Off agit folk, with hedis hore and olde ;
        ȝone were the folke that neuer changë wold
    In lufe, bot trewly seruit him alway,
    In euery age, vnto thaire ending-day.

84 For fro the tyme that thai coud vnderstand
        The exercise, of lufis craft the cure,
    Was noñ on lyve that toke so moch on hand
        For lufis sake, nor langer did endure
        In lufis seruice ; for man, I the assure,
    Quhen thay of ȝouth ressauit had the fill,
    ȝit In thaire age thañ lakkit no gude will.

85 Here bene also of suich as In counsailis
        And all thar dedis, were to venus trewe ;
    Here bene the princis, faucht the grete batailis,
        In mynd of quhom ar maid the bukis newe,
        Here beñ the poetis that the sciencis knewe,
    Throwout the warld, of lufe in thaire suete layes,
    Suich as Ouide and Omere in thaire dayes.

86 And efter thame dowñ In the next[ë] stage,
        There as thou seis the ȝong[ë] folkis pleye :
    Lo ! thise were thay that, in thaire myddill age,
        Seruandis were to lufe in mony weye,
        And diuersely happinnit for to deye ;
    Sum soroufully, for wanting of thare makis,
    And sum in armes for thaire ladyes sakis.

            [1] MS. ȝonder there ; but there is not wanted.

87 And othir eke by othir diuerse chance,
　　As happin folk all day, as ȝe may se;
　Sum for dispaire, without recouerance;
　　　Sum for desyre, surmounting thaire degree;
　　　Sum for dispite and othir Inmytee;
　Sum for vnkyndënes without a quhy;
　Sum for to moch, and sum for Ielousye.

88 And efter this, vpon ȝone stage [a]douñ,
　　Tho that thou seis stond in capis wyde;
　Ȝone were quhilum folk of religiouñ,
　　　That from the warld thaire gouernance did hide,
　　　And frely seruit lufe on euery syde
　In secrete, with thaire bodyis and thaire gudis.
　And lo! quhy so thai hingen douñ thaire hudis:

89 For though that thai were hardy at assay,
　　And did him seruice quhilum priuely,
　Ȝit to the warldis eye It semyt nay;
　　　So was thaire seruice half[del] cowardy:
　　　And for thay first forsuke him opynly,
　And efter that thereof had repenting,
　For schame thaire hudis oure thaire eyne thay hyng.

90 And seis thou now ȝone multitude, on rawe
　　Standing, behynd ȝone trauerse of delyte?
　Sum bene of tham that haldin were full lawe,
　　　And take by frendis, nothing thay to wyte,
　　　In ȝouth from lufe Into the cloistere quite;
　And for that cause are cummyn recounsilit,
　On thame to pleyne that so tham had begilit.

91 And othir bene amongis thame also,
　　That cummyn ar to court, on lufe to pleyne,
　For he thaire bodyes had bestowit so,

Quhare bothe thaire hertes gruch[en] ther-ageyne ;
For quhich, In all thaire dayes, soth to seyne,
Quhen othir lyvit In Ioye and [in] plesance,
Thaire lyf was noght bot care and repentance ;

92 And quhare thaire hertis gevin were and set,
    Coplit[1] with othir that coud noght accord ;
Thus were thai wrangit that did no forfet,
    Departing thame that neuer wold discord ;
    Off ʒong[ë] ladies faire, and mony lord,
That thus by maistry were fro thair chose dryve,
Full redy were thaire playntis there to gyve."

93 And othir also I sawe compleynyng there
    Vpon fortune and hir grete variance,
That quhere In loue so wele they coplit were,
    With thaire suete makis coplit in plesance,
    Sche[2] sodeynly maid thaire disseuerance,
And tuke thame of this warldis companye,
Withoutin cause, there was non othir quhy.

94 And in a chiere of estate besyde,
    With wingis bright, all plumyt, bot his face,
There sawe I sitt the blynd[ë] god Cupide,
    With bow In hand, that bent full redy was,
    And by him hang thre arowis In a cas,
Off quhich the hedis grundyn were full ryght,
Off diuerse metals forgit faire and bryght.

95 And with the first, that hedit is of gold,
    He smytis soft, and that has esy cure ;
The secund was of siluer, mony fold
    Wers than the first, and harder auenture ;
    The thrid, of stele, is schot without recure ;

---

[1] MS. Were coplit (*but* were *can be understood*).   [2] MS. So.

And on his long[ë] ȝalow lokk*is* schene
A chaplet had he all of levis grene.

96 And In a retrete lytill of compas,
   Depeyntit all w*ith* sighis wond*er* sad,
Nog*ht* suich sighis as hertis doith manace,
   Bot suich as dooth lufar*is* to be glad,
   Fond I ven*us* vpon hir bed, th*at* had
A mantill cast ou*er* hir schuldris quhite :
Thus clothit was the goddesse of delyte.

97 Stude at the dure fair-calling, hir vschere,
   That coude his office doon In co*n*nyng wis*e*,
And secretee, hir thrifty chamberere,
   That besy was In tyme to do s*er*uis*e*,
   And othir mo th*at* I can nog*ht* on avis*e* ;
And on hir hede, of rede rosis full suete,
A chapellet sche had, fair*e*, fresch, and mete.

98 W*ith* quaking hert astonate of that sight,
   Vnnethis wist I quhat th*at* I suld seyne ;
Bot at the last[ë] febily as I myg*ht*,
   W*ith* my handis on bothe my kneis tueyne,
   There I begouth my car*is* to compleyne ;
W*ith* ane humble and lam*en*table chere
Thus salute I that goddess*e* bryg*ht* and clere :

99 " HYE quene of lufe ! sterr*e* of beneuolence!
       Pitous*e* princes, and planet m*er*ciable!
   Appesar*e* of malice and violence !
       By vertew pur*e* of ȝo*ur* aspectis hable,
       Vnto ȝour*e* grace lat now beñ acceptable
   My pur*e* request, th*at* can no forthir gone
   To seken help, bot vnto ȝow allone !

100 As ȝe that bene the socoure and suete well
    Off remedye, of carefull hertes cure,
And, in the hugë weltering wawis fell
    Off lufis rage, blisfull havin and sure;
    O anker and keye of oure gude auenture,
ȝe haue ȝour man with his gude will conquest:
Merci, therefore, and bring his hert to rest!

101 ȝe knaw the cause of all my peynes smert
    Bet than my-self, and all myn auenture
ȝe may conuoye, and as ȝow list, conuert
    The hardest hert that formyt hath nature:
    Sen in ȝour handis all hale lyith my cure,
Haue pitee now, o bryght blisfull goddesse,*
Off ȝour pure man, and rew on his distresse!

102 And though I was vnto ȝour lawis strange,
    By ignorance, and noght by felonye,
And that ȝour grace now likit hath to change
    My hert, to seruen ȝow perpetualye,
    Forgeue all this, and shapith remedye
To sauen me of ȝour benignë grace,
Or do me steruen furth-with in this place.

103 And with the stremes of ȝour percyng lyght
    Conuoy my hert, that is so wo begone,
Ageyne vnto that suetë hevinly sight,
    That I, within the wallis cald as stone,
    So suetly saw on morow walk and gone,
Law in the gardyn, ryght tofore myn eye:
Now, merci, quene! and do me noght to deye."

104 Thir wordis said, my spirit in dispaire,
    A quhile I stynt, abiding efter grace:
And there-with-all hir cristall eyën faire

Sche[1] kest asyde, and efter that a space,
Benignëly sche turnyt has hir face
Towardis me full plesantly conueide;
And vnto me ryght in this wise sche seide:

105 " 3ong man, the cause of all thyne Inward sorowe
Is noght vnknawin to my deite,
And thy request, bothe now and eke toforowe,
Quhen thou first maid professioun to me;
Sen of my grace I haue inspirit the
To knawe my lawe, contynew furth, for oft,
There as I mynt full sore, I smyte[2] bot soft.

106 Paciently thou tak thyne auenture,
This will my soñ Cupide, and so will I,
He can the stroke, to me langis the cure
Quhen I se tyme, and therefor humily[3]
Abyde, and serue, and lat gude hope the gye:
Bot, for I haue thy forehede here present,
I will the schewe the more of myn entent.

107 This Is to say, though It to me pertene
In lufis lawe the septre to gouerne,
That the effectis of my bemes schene
Has thaire aspectis by ordynance eterne,
With otheris bynd and mynes to discerne,[4]
Quhilum in thingis bothe to cum and gone,
That langis noght to me, to writh allone;

108 As in thyne awin case now may thou se,
For-quhy lo, that [by] otheris Influence
Thy persone standis noght In libertee;
Quharefore, though I geve the beneuolence,
It standis noght 3it In myn aduertence,

---

[1] MS. Me.
[2] Full *is written after* smyte, *but is crossed through.*
[3] MS. huily. [4] *Corrupt; see the note.*

Till certeyne coursis endit be and ronne,
Quhill of trew seruis thow have hir graice I-wone.

109 And ʒit, considering the nakitnesse
      Bothe of thy wit, thy persone, and thy myght,
    It is no mach, of thyne vnworthynesse
      To hir hie birth, estate, and beautee bryght:
      Als like ʒe bene, as day is to the nyght;
    Or sek-cloth is vnto fyne cremesye;
    Or doken[1] to the freschë dayesye.

110 Vnlike the mone Is to the sonnë schene;
      Eke Ianuarye is [vn]like to[2] may;
    Vnlike the cukkow to the phylomene;
      Thaire tabartis ar noght bothe maid of array;[3]
      Vnlike the crow is to the papë-Iay;
    Vnlike, In goldsmythis werk, a fischis eye
    To peire[4] with perll, or maked be so heye.

111 As I haue said, [now] vnto me belangith
      Specialy the cure of thy seknesse;
    Bot now thy matere so in balance hangith,
      That It requerith, to thy sekernesse,
      The help of othir mo that[5] bene goddes,
    And haue In thame the menes and the lore,
    In this matere to schorten with thy sore.

112 And for thou sall se wele that I entend,
      Vn-to thy help, thy welefare to preserue,
    The streight[ë] weye thy spirit will I send
      To the goddesse that clepit is Mynerue,
      And se that thou hir hestis wele conserue,

For in this case sche may be thy supplye,
And put thy hert in rest, als wele as I.

113 Bot, for the way is vncouth vnto the,
    There as hir duelling is and hir soiurne,
  I will that gude hope seruand to the be,
    3oure alleris frend, to let[të] the to murn,
    Be thy condyt and gyde till thou returne,
  And hir besech, that sche will, in thy nede,
  Hir counsele geve to thy welefare and spede.

114 And that sche will, as langith hir office,
    Be thy gude lady, help and counseiloure,
  And to the schewe hir rype and gude auise,
    Throw quhich thou may, be processe and laboure,
    Atteyne vnto that glad and goldyn floure,
  That thou wald haue so fayn with all thy hart.
  And forthir-more, sen thou hir seruand art,

115 Quhen thou descendis doun to ground ageyne,
    Say to the men that there bene resident,
  How long think thay to stand in my disdeyne,
    That in my lawis bene so negligent
    From day to day, and list tham noght repent,
  Bot breken louse, and walken at thaire large?
  Is nocht eft none[1] that thereof gevis charge?

116 And for," quod sche, "the angir and the smert
    Off thaire vnkyndënesse dooth me constreyne,
  My femynyne and wofull tender hert,
    That than I wepe ; and, to a token pleyne,
    As of my teris cummyth all this reyne,
  That 3e se on the ground so fast ybete
  Fro day to day, my turment is so grete.

----

[1] MS. Is non (*corrected to* nocht) eft, *with* none *above.*

117 And quhen I wepe, and stynten othir quhile,
       For pacience that is in womanhede,
     Than all my wrath and rancoure I exile;
         And of my cristall teris that bene schede,
         The hony flouris growen vp and sprede,
     That preyen men, [as] In thaire flouris wise,
     Be trewe of lufe, and worschip my seruise.

118 And eke, In takin of this pitouse tale,
       Quhen so my teris dropen on the ground,
     In thaire nature the lytill birdis smale
         Styntith thaire song, and murnyth for that stound,
         And all the lightis In the hevin round
     Off my greuance haue suich compacience,
     That from the ground they hiden thaire presence.

119 And ʒit In tokenyng forthir of this thing,
       Quhen flouris springis, and freschest bene of hewe,
     And that the birdis on the twistis sing,
         At thilkë tyme ay gynnen folk renewe[1]
         That seruis vnto loue, as ay is dewe,
     Most commonly has ay his obseruance,
     And of thaire sleuth tofore haue repentance.

120 Thus maist thou seyne, that myn effectis grete,
       Vnto the quhich ʒe aught and maist weye,[2]
     No lyte offense, to sleuth is [al] forget :
         And therefore In this wisë to tham seye,
         As I the here haue bid[den], and conueye
     The matere all the better tofore said ;
     Thus sall on the my chargë bene Ilaid.

121 Say on than, ‘quhare Is becummyn, for schame!
       The songis new, the fresch carolis and dance,
     The lusty lyf, the mony change of game,

---

[1] MS. folk to renewe (*wrongly*).   [2] *For* aught and *read* aughten.

The fresche array, the lusty contenance,
The besy awayte, the hertly obseruance,
That quhilum was amongis thame so ryf?
Bid tham repent in tyme, and mend thaire lyf:

122 Or I sall, with my fader old Saturne,
        And with al hale oure hevinly alliance,
    Oure glad aspectis from thame writh and turne,
        That all the warld sall waile thaire gouernance.
        Bid thame be tyme that thai haue repentance,
    And [with] thaire hertis hale renew my lawe;
    And I my hand fro beting sall withdrawe.

123 This is to say, contynew in my seruise,
        Worschip my law, and my name magnifye,
    That am 3our hevin and 3our paradise;
        And I 3our confort here sall multiplye,
        And, for 3our meryt here, perpetualye
    Ressaue I sall 3our saulis of my grace,
    To lyve with me as goddis In this place.'"

124 With humble thank, and all the reuerence
        That feble wit and connyng may atteyne,
    I tuke my leue; and from hir [hy] presence,
        Gude hope and I to-gider, bothë tueyne,
        Departit are, and, schortly for to seyne,
    He hath me led [the] redy wayis ryght
    Vnto Mineruis palace, faire and bryght.

125 Quhare as I fand, full redy at the 3ate,
        The maister portare, callit pacience,
    That frely lete vs in, vnquestionate;
        And there we sawe the perfyte excellence,
        The said renewe, the state, the reuerence,
    The strenth, the beautee, and the ordour digne
    Off hir court riall, noble and benigne.

126 And straught vnto the presence sodeynly
 Off dame Min*er*ue, the pacient goddess*e*,
Gude hope my gydë led me redily;
 To quhom anoñ, w*ith* dredefull humylness*e*,
 Off my cu*m*myng the caus*e* I gan expresse,
And all the process*e* hole, vnto the end,
Off ven*us* charge, as likit hir to send.

127 Off quhich ryg*h*t thus hir ansuer*e* was i*n* bref:
 "My soñ, I haue wele herd, and vnd*er*stond,
Be thy reherse, the mater*e* of thy gref,
 And thy request to procur*e*, and to fonde
 Off thy pe*n*nance sum confort at my hond,
Be counsele of thy lady ven*us* clere,
To be w*ith* hir thyne help In this matere.

128 Bot in this cas*e* thou sall wele knawe and witt,
 Thou may thy hert[ë] ground on suich a wis*e*,
That thy laboure will be bot lytill quit;
 And thou may set It In [an]othir wis*e*,
 That wil be to the grete worschip and pris*e*,
And gif thou durst vnto that way enclyne,
I will the geve my lore and disciplyne.

129 Lo, my gude sone, this Is als mich to seyne,
 As, gif thy lufe sett allut*er*ly
Of nycë lust, thy trauail is in veyne;
 And so the end sall turne of thy folye
 To payne and repe*n*tance; lo, wate thou quhy?
Gif the ne list on lufe thy v*er*tew set,
Vertu sall be the caus*e* of thy forfet.

130 Tak him befor*e* In all thy gou*er*nance,
 That in his hand the stere has of ȝou all,
And pray vnto his hyë p*ur*ueyance,

Thy lufe to gye, and on him traist and call,
That corner-stone and ground is of the wall,
That failis noght, and trust, withoutin drede,
Vnto thy purpose sone he sall the lede.

131 For lo, the werk that first Is foundit sure,
May better bere a pace and hyare be,
Than othir wise, and langere sall endure,
Be monyfald, this may thy resoun see,
And stronger to defend aduersitee :
Ground [thou] thy werk, therefore, vpon the stone,
And thy desire sall forthward with the gone.

132 Be trewe, and meke, and stedfast in thy thoght,
And diligent hir merci to procure,
Noght onely in thy word ; for word is noght,
Bot gif thy werk and all thy besy cure
Accord thereto ; and vtrid be mesure,
The place, the houre, the maner, and the wise,
Gif mercy sall admitten thy seruise.

133 All thing has tyme, thus sais Ecclesiaste ;
And wele is him that his tyme wel[1] abit :
Abyde thy time ; for he that can bot haste,
Can noght of hap, the wise man It writ ;
And oft gude fortune flourish with gude wit :
Quharefore, gif thou will [ay] be wele fortunyt,
Lat wisedom ay [vn]to thy will be Iunyt.

134 Bot there be mony of so brukill sort,
That feynis treuth In lufe for a quhile,
And setten all thaire wittis and disport,
The sely Innocent woman to begyle,
And so to wynne thaire lustis with a wile ;

[1] MS. wil.

C

Suich feynit treuth is all bot trechorye,
Vnder the vmbre of hid[1] ypocrisye.

135 For as the foulere quhistlith in his throte
Diuersely, to counterfete the brid,
And feynis mony a suete and strangë note
That in the busk for his desate is hid,
Till sche be fast lokin[2] his net amyd ;
Ryght so the fatoure, the false theif, I say,
With suete tresoun oft wynnith thus his pray.

136 Fy on all suich ! fy on thaire doubilnesse !
Fy on thaire lust and bestly appetite !
Thaire wolfis hertis, in lambis liknesse ;
Thaire thoughtis blak, hid vnder wordis quhite ;
Fy on thaire laboure ! fy on thaire delyte !
That feynen outward all to hir honour,
And in thaire hert hir worschip wold deuoure.

137 So hard It is to trusten now on dayes
The warld, It is so double and inconstant,
Off quhich the suth is kid be mony assayes ;
More pitee is ; for quhich the remanant,
That menen wele, and ar noght variant,
For otheris gilt ar[3] suspect of vntreuth,
And hyndrit oft, and treuely that is reuth.

138 Bot gif the hert be groundit ferm and stable
In goddis law, thy purpose to atteyne,
Thy laboure is to me [ful] agreable ;
And my full help, with counsele trew and pleyne,
I will the schewe, and this is the certeyne ;
Opyn thy hert, therefore, and lat me se
Gif thy remede be pertynent to me."

[1] MS. heid (obscurely written; see hid in st. 136).
[2] MS. lok in.   [3] MS. and (copied from the line above).

139 " Madame," quod I, " sen It is 30ur plesance
    That I declare the kynd of my loving,
  Treuely and gude, withoutin variance,
      In lufe that floure abufe all othir thing ;
      And wold bene he that to hir worschipping
  Myght ought auaile, be him that starf on rude,
  And nouthir spare for trauaile, lyf, nor gude.

140 And, forthirmore, as touching the nature
      Off my lufing, to worschip or to blame,
  I darre wele say, and there-in me assure,
      For ony gold, that ony wight can name,
      Wald[1] I be he that suld of hir gude fame
  Be blamischere In ony point or wyse,
  For wele nor wo, quhill my lyf may suffise.

141 This Is theffect trewly of myn entent,
      Touching the suete that smertis me so sore,
  Giff this be faynt, I can It noght repent,
      All though my lyf suld forfaut be therefore,
      Blisful princes ! I can seye 30u no more ;
  Bot so desire my wittis dooth compace,
  More Ioy in erth kepe I noght bot 30ur grace."

142 " Desire," quod sche, " I nyl It noght deny,
      So thou It ground and set in cristin wise ;
  And therefore, soñ, opyn thy hert playnly."
      " Madame," quod I, " trew withoutin fantise,
      That day sall neuer be I sall[2] vp-rise,
  For my delyte to couate the plesance,
  That may hir worschip putten In balance.

143 For oure all thing, lo, this were my gladnesse,
      To sene the freschë beautee of hir face ;

[1] *Read* Nold.   [2] MS. sall I neuer (*leaving the line incomplete*).

And gif I [1] myg*h*t des*e*ruë, be process*e*,
 For my grete lufe and treuth, to stond in grace,
 Hir worschip sauf, lo, here the blisfull cace
That I wold ask, and there[vn]to attend,
For my most Ioye vnto my lyfis end."

144 " Now wele," qu*o*d sche, " and sen th*a*t It is so,
 That In v*e*rtew thy lufe is set w*i*t*h* treuth,
To helpen the I will be one of tho
 From hen[ne]sforth, and hertly w*i*t*h*out sleuth,
 Off thy distress*e* and excess*e* to haue reuth
That has thy hert; I will [hir] pray full fair*e*,
That fortune be no more ther*e*to contrair*e*.

145 For suth It is, th*a*t all ʒe creatur*i*s,
 Quhich vnd*e*r vs beneth haue ʒo*u*r duellyng,
Ressauen diu*e*rs*e*ly ʒo*u*r aue*n*tur*i*s,
 Off quhich the cur*e* and pri*n*cipall melling
 Apperit is, w*i*t*h*outin repellyng,
Onely to hir th*a*t has the cuttis two
In hand, bothe of ʒo*u*r wele and of ʒo*u*r wo.

146 And how so be [it], th*a*t sum clerk*i*s trete,
 That all ʒo*u*r chancë causit Is tofore
Heigh In the hevin, by quhois effect*i*s grete
 ʒe movit ar*e* to wrething less*e* or more,
 Quhare [2] In the warld, th*u*s calling th*a*t ther*e*fore
' Fortune,' and so th*a*t the diu*e*rsitee
Off thair*e* wirking suld caus*e* necessitee ;

147 Bot othir clerk*i*s halden, th*a*t the man
 Has In him-self the chos*e* and libertee
To caus*e* his awin fortune, how or quhan
 That him best lest, and no necessitee
 Was In the hevi*n* at his natiuitee,

---

[1] MS. It.   [2] *Read* Thar.

Bot ȝit the thingis happin in commune
Efter purpose, so cleping thame ' fortune.'

148 And quhare a persone has tofore knawing
Off It that is to fall[en] purposely,
Lo, fortune is bot wayke in suich a thing,
Thou may wele wit, and here ensample quhy;
To god, that [1] is the first[ë] cause onely
Off euery thing, there may no fortune fall :
And quhy? for he foreknawin is of all.

149 And therefore thus I say to this sentence;
Fortune is most and strangest euermore,
Quhare lest foreknawing or intelligence
Is in the man; and, sone, of wit or lore
Sen thou are wayke and feble, lo, therefore,
The more thou art in dangere and commune
With hir, that clerkis clepen so fortune.

150 Bot for the sake, and at the reuerence
Off venus clere, as I the said tofore,
I haue of thy distresse compacience ;
And in confort and relesche of thy sore,
The schewit [haue] here myn avise therefore ;
Pray fortune help, for mich vnlikly thing
Full oft about sche sodeynly dooth bring.

151 Now go thy way, and haue gude mynde vpoñ
Quhat I haue said In way of thy doctryne."
" I sall, madame," quod I [2] ; and ryght anoñ
I tuke my leve :—als straught as ony lyne,
With-in a beme, that fro the contree dyvine
Sche, percyng throw the firmament, extendit,
To ground ageyne my spirit is descendit.

[1] MS. It (put for yt).   [2] MS. he.

152 Quhare, In a lusty plane, tuke I my way,
      Endlang a ryuer, plesant to behold,
    Enbroudin all with freschë flouris gay,
        Quhare, throu the grauel, bryght as ony gold,
        The cristall water ran so clere and cold,
      That, In myn erë maid contynualy
      A maner souñ, mellit with armony;

153 That full of lytill fischis by the brym,
        Now here, now there, with bakkis blewe as lede,
    Lap and playit, and In a rout can swym
        So prattily, and dressit tham to sprede
        Thaire curall fynnis, as the ruby rede,
      That In the sonnë on thaire scalis bryght
      As gesserant ay glitterit In my sight:

154 And by this Ilkë ryuer-syde alawe
        Ane hyë way [thar] fand I like to bene,
    On quhich, on euery syde, a long[ë] rawe
        Off treis saw I, full of leuis grene,
        That full of fruyte delitable were to sene,
      And also, as It come vnto my mind,
      Off bestis sawe I mony diuerse kynd:

155 The lyoun king, and his fere lyonesse;
        The pantere, like vnto the smaragdyne;
    The lytill squerell, full of besynesse;
        The slawë ase, the druggare beste of pyne;
        The nycë ape; the werely porpapyne;
      The percyng lynx; the lufare vnicorne,
      That voidis venym with his euour horne.

156 There sawe I dresse him new out of [his] haunt
        The fery tigere, full of felonye;
      The dromydare; the standar oliphant;

The wyly fox, the wedowis Inemye ;
  The clymbar*e* gayte ; the elk for alblastrye ;
The herknere bore ; the holsum grey for hort*is* ;
  The hair*e* also, th*a*t oft gooth to the wortis.

157 The bugill, drawar*e* by his hornis grete ;
  The martrik, sable, the foyn3ee, and mony mo ;
The chalk-quhite ermyn, tippit as the Iete ;
  The riall hert, the conyng, and the ro ;
    The wolf, th*a*t of the murthir no*gh*t say[is] "ho ! "
The lesty beu*er*, and the ravin bare ;
For chamelot, the camel full of hare ;

158 With mony añ othir beste diu*erse* and strange,
  That cu*m*myth no*gh*t as now vnto my mynd.
Bot now to p*ur*pose,—straucht furth the range
  I held a way, our*e*-hailing in my mynd
    From quheñs I come, and quhare th*a*t I suld fynd
Fortune, the goddess*e* ; vnto quhom In hye
Gude hope, my gyde, has led me sodeynly ;

159 And at the last, behalding thus asyde,
  A round place [y]wallit haue I found ;
In myddis quhare eftsone I haue [a]spide
  Fortune, the goddess*e*, hufing on the gro*u*nd ;
    And ry*gh*t befor*e* hir fete, of compas round,
A quhele, on quhich [than] cleu*er*ing I sye
A multitude of folk befor*e* my*n* eye.

160 And ane surcote sche werit long that tyde,
  That semyt [vn]to me of diu*erse* hewis,
Quhilum thus, quhen sche wald [hir] turñ asyde,
  Stude this goddess*e* of fortune and [of glewis] ;
    A chapellet, wi*th* mony fresche anewis.

Sche had vpon her hed; and w*ith* this hong
A mantill on hir schuldris, large and long,

161 That furrit was w*ith* ermyn full quhite,
  Degoutit w*ith* the self In spottis blake :
And quhilum In hir chier*e* thus a lyte[1]
  Louring sche was; and thus sone It wold slake,
  And sodeynly a man*er* smylyng make,
And sche were glad; [for] at one contenance
Sche held no*gh*t, bot [was] ay in variance.

162 And vnd*er*neth the quhelë sawe I there
  Ane vgly pit, [was] depe as ony helle,
That to behald ther*e*on I quoke for fere;
  Bot o thing herd I, th*at* quho ther*e*-In fell
  Com*e* no more vp agane, tidingis to telle;
Off quhich, astonait of that ferefull sy*gh*t,
I ne wist quhat to done, so was I fricht.

163 Bot for to se the sudayn welt*er*ing
  Off that Ilk quhele, th*at* sloppar*e* was to hold,
It semyt vnto my wit a strangë[2] thing,
  So mony I sawe th*at* than clymben wold,
  And failit foting, and to gro*u*nd wer*e* rold;
And othir eke, th*at* sat aboue on hye,
Wer*e* ou*er*thrawe In twinklyng of añ eye.

164 And on the quhele was lytill void space,
  Wele nere our*e*-straught fro lawë [vn]to hye;
And they were war*e* that long[ë] sat In place,
  So tolt*er* quhilum did sche It to-wrye;
  There was bot clymbe[n] and ry*gh*t dounward hye,
And sum were eke th*at* fallyng had [so] sore,
There for to clymbe thair*e* corage was no more.

[1] MS. a*l*yte.   [2] MS. strong.

165 I sawe also that, quhere [as] sum were slungin,
    Be quhirlyng of the quhele, vnto the ground,
  Full sudaynly sche hath [thaim] vp ythrungin,
    And set thame on agane full sauf and sound:
    And euer I sawe a new[e] swarm abound,
  That [thought] to clymbe vpward vpon the quhele,
  In stede of thame that myght no langer rele.

166 And at the last, In presen[c]e of thame all
    That stude about, sche clepit me be name;
  And therewith apon kneis gan I fall
    Full sodaynly hailsing, abaist for schame;
    And, smylyng thus, sche said to me in game;
  "Quhat dois thou here? quho has the hider sent?
  Say on anoñ, and tell me thyñ entent.

167 I se wele, by thy chere and contenance,
    There is sum thing that lyis the on hert,
  It stant noght with the as thou wald, perchance?"
    "Madame," quod I, "for lufe Is all the smert
    That euer I fele, endlang and ouerthwert;
  Help, of 30ur grace, me wofull wrechit wight,
  Sen me to cure 3e powere haue and myght."

168 "Quhat help," quod sche, "wold thou that I ordeyne,
    To bring[en] the vnto thy hertis desire?"
  "Madame," quod I, "bot that 30ur grace dedeyne,
    Off 30ur grete myght, my wittis to enspire,
    To win the well that slokin may the fyre
  In quhich I birn; a, goddesse fortunate!
  Help now my game, that is in poynt to mate."

169 "Off mate?" quod sche, "o! verray sely wrech,
    I se wele by thy dedely coloure pale,
  Thou art to feble of thy-self to streche

Vpon my quhele, to clymbe[n] or to hale
Withoutin help ; for thou has fundin stale
This mony day, wi*th*outin werdis wele,
And wantis now thy veray hertis hele.

170 Wele maistow be a wrechit man [y]callit,
   That wantis the confort suld[1] thy hert[ë] glade ;
And has all thing within thy hert[ë] stallit,
   That may thy ȝouth oppressen or defade.
   Though thy begy*n*nyng hath bene retrograde,
Be froward opposyt quhare till aspert,
Now sall thai turñ, and luke[n] on the dert."

171 And ther*with*-all vnto the quhele In hye
   Sche hath me led, and bad me lere to clymbe,
Vpon the quhich I steppit sudaynly,
   "Now hald thy grippis," q*uo*d sche, "for thy tyme,
   An*e* hour*e* and more It ry*n*nis ou*er* prime ;
To count the hole, the half is ner*e* away ;
Spend wele, ther*efore*, the remanant of the day.

172 Ensample," q*uo*d sche, "tak of this tofore,
   That fro my quhele be rollit as a ball ;
For the nature of It is eu*er*more,
   After ane hicht, to vale and geue a fall,
   Thus, quhen me likith, vp or douñ to fall.
Fare wele," q*uo*d sche, and by the ere me toke
So ernestly, that ther*with*all I woke.

173 O besy goste ! ay flikering to and fro,
   That neu*er* art In quiet nor In rest,
Till thou cu*m* to that place th*a*t thou cam fro,
   Quhich is thy first and verray prop*er* nest :
   From day to day so sore here artow drest,

---

[1] MS. th*a*t suld; *but* th*a*t *is not wanted.*

That w*ith* thy flesche ay walking art in trouble,
And sleping eke ; of pyne so has thou double.

174 Couert my-self all this mene I to loke,
　　Though th*a*t my spirit vexit was tofore
In sueu[en]yng, alssone as eu*er* I woke,
　　By twenty[1] fold It was In trouble more,
　　Bethinking me w*ith* sighing hert and sore,
That [I] nañ othir thingis bot dremes had,
Nor sek*er*nes, my spirit w*ith* to glad.

175 And ther*ewith* sone I dressit me to rys*e*,
　　Fulfild of tho*g*ht, pyne, and adu*er*sitee ;
And to my-self I said vpon[2] this wis*e* ;
　　　　A ! m*er*ci, lord ! quhat will ʒe do w*ith* me ?
　　　　Quhat lyf is this ? quhare hath my spirit be ?[3]
Is this of my for*e*tho*g*ht Impressiou*n*,
Or Is It from the hevin a visiou*n*?

176 And gif ʒe goddis, of ʒour*e* p*ur*uiance,
　　Haue schewit this for my reconforting,
In relesche of my furious*e* pe*n*nance,
　　I ʒow beseke full hu*m*ily of this thing,
　　That of ʒour*e* grace I my*g*ht haue more takenyng,
Gif It sal be as in my slepe before
ʒe shewit haue : and forth, w*ith*outin more,

177 In hye vnto the wyndow gan I walk,
　　Moving within my spirit of this sight,
Quhare sodeynly a t*ur*tur*e*, quhite as c[h]alk,
　　So evinly vpon my hand gan ly*g*ht,
　　And vnto me sche t*ur*nyt hir full ry*g*ht,

---

[1] MS. xxtj.　　　　　　　　　　　　　　　[2] MS. In.
[3] *This line and the preceding are transposed in the MS.; but they
are marked* a *and* b *respectively.*

Off quham the chere in hir birdis aport
Gave me In hert[ë] kalendis of confort.

178 This[1] fair[ë] bird ry*ght* In hir bill gañ hold
 Of red Iorofflis with thair stalkis grene
A fair[ë] branche, quhare writtin was with gold,
 On euery list, with[2] branchis bry*ght* and schene
 In compas fair, full plesandly to sene,
A plane sentence, quhich, as I cañ deui*se*
And haue In mynd, said ry*ght* [vp]oñ this wi*se*.

179 "Awak! awake! I bring, lufar, I bring
 The newis glad, that blisfull beñ and sure
Of thy confort; now lauch, and play, and syng,
 That art besid so glad añ auenture;
 For In the hevyn decretit is the cure;"
And vnto me the flouris fair present:
With wyng*is* spred, hir wayis furth sche went.

180 Quhilk vp a-noñ I tuke, and as I gess*e*,
 Añe hundreth tymes, or I forthir went,
I haue It red, with hert[ë]full glaidnes*e*;
 And, half with hope, and half w*ith* dred, It hent,
 And at my beddis hed, with gud entent,
I haue It fair[ë] py*n*nit vp, and this
First takyñ was of all my help and bliss*e*.

181 The quhich[ë] treuly efter, day be day,
 That all my witt*is* maistrit had tofore,
From[3] hen[ne]sferth the paynis did away.
 And schortly, so wele fortune has hir bore,
 To quikin treuly day by day my lore,
To my larges that I am cu*m*in agayñ,
To bliss*e* with hir that is my souirane.

---

[1] *Stanzas* 178 (l. 1) to 192 (l. 5) *are in a different hand.*
[2] MS. witht.   [3] MS. Quhich, *wrongly; see* st. 69, 144.

182 Bot for als moche as sum micht think or seyne,
    Quhat nedis me, apoun̄ so litill evyn̄,
  To writt all this? I ansuere thus ageyne,—
    Quho that from hell war croppin[1] onys In hevin,
    Wald efter O thank for Ioy mak vj or vij :
  And euery wicht his awin suete or sore
  Has maist In mynde : I can say ʒou no more.

183 Eke quho may In this lyfe haue more plesañce,
    Than cum to largesse from̄ thraldom and peyne,
  And by the mene of luffis Ordinance,
    That has so mony In his goldin cheyne?
    Quhich thinkis[2] to wyn̄ his hertis souereyne,
  Quho suld me wite to write thar-of, lat se !
  Now sufficiante Is my felicitee.

184 Beseching vnto fair venus abufe,
    For all my brethir that bene In this place,
  This Is to seyne, that seruandis ar to lufe,
    And of his lady can no thank purchase,
    His paine relesch, and sone to stand In grace,
  Boith to his worschip and to his first ese ;
  So that It hir and resoun̄ noḡht displese :

185 And eke for tham̄ that ar noḡht entrit Inne
    The dañce of lufe, bot thidder-wart on̄ way,
  In gudë tyme and sely to begynne
    Thair prentissehed, and forthir-more I pray
    For thame that passit ben the mony affray[3]
  In lufe, and cummyn[4] ar to full plesañce,
  To graunt tham̄ all, lo ! gude perseuerañce :

186 And eke I pray for all the hertis dull,
    That lyven̄ here In sleūth and Ignorance,
  And has no curage at the rose to pull,

---

[1] MS. coppin, *with* r *above, after* c.   [2] MS. this.
[3] This line and the preceding are transposed in the MS.
[4] MS. cunnyng.

Thair lif to mend and thair saulis auance
With thair suete lore, and bring tham to gude chance ;
And quho that will no*ght* for this p*r*ayer turñ,
Quhen thai wald faynest speid, that thai may spurñ.

187 To Rekyñ of euery thing the circumstañce,
As hapnit me quheñ lesseñ gan my sore
Of my rancoure and [al my] wofull chañce.
It war to long, I lat It be tharefor.
And thus this floure, I can seye [ʒou] no more,
So hertly has vnto my help attendit,
That from the deth hir mañ sche has defendit.

188 And eke the goddis mercifull virking,
For my long pañe and trewe s*er*uice In lufe,
That has me gevin halely my*n* asking,
Quhich has my hert for euir sett abufe
In perfyte Ioy, that neuir may remufe,
Bot onely deth : of quhom, In laud and pris*e*,
With thankfull hert I say richt In this wis*e* :—

189 "Blissit mot be the [heyë] goddis all,
So fair that glitt*er*en In the firmament !
And blissit be thare my*ght* celestiall,
That haue convoyit hale, with one assent,
My lufe, and to [so] glade a consequent !
And thankit be fortunys exiltree
And quhele,[1] that thus so wele has quhirlit me.

190 Thankit mot be, and fair and lufe befall
The nychtingale, that, with so gud entent,
Sang thare of lufe the not*is* suete and small,
Quhair my fair hertis lady was p*r*eseñt,
Hir with to glad, or that sche forthir went !
And thou gerafloure, mot I-thankit be
All othir flour*is* for the lufe of the !

                    [1] MS. quhile.

191 And thankit be the fair[ë] castell wall,
    Quhare as I quhilom lukit furth and lent.
  Thankit mot be the sanctis marciall,
    That me first causit hath this accident.
    Thankit mot be the grenë bewis bent,
  Throu quhom, and vnder, first fortunyt me
  My hertis hele, and my confort to be.

192 For to the presence suete and delitable,
    Rycht of this floure that full Is of plesance,
  By processe and by menys fauorable,
    First of the blisfull goddis purueyance,
    And syne throu long and trew contynuance
  Of veray faith In lufe and trew seruice,
  I cum am, and [ȝit][1] forthir In this wise.

193 Vnworthy, lo, bot onely of hir grace,
    In lufis ȝok, that esy is and sure,
  In guerdoun [eke] of all my lufis space,
    Sche hath me tak, hir humble creature.
    And thus befell my blisfull auenture,
  In ȝouth of lufe, that now, from day to day,
  Flourith ay newe, and ȝit forthir, I say.

194 Go litill tretise, nakit of eloquence,
    Causing simplese and pouertee to wit;
  And pray the reder to haue pacience
    Of thy defaute, and to supporten It,
    Of his gudnese thy brukilnese to knytt,
  And his tong for to reule[n] and to stere,
  That thy defautis helit may ben here.

195 Allace! and gif thou cummyst In[2] presence,
    Quhare-as of blame faynest thou wald be quite,
  To here thy rude and crukit eloquens,

---

[1] See st. 193, last line.   [2] MS. In the presence.

Quho sal be[1] thare to pray for thy remyt?
No wicht, bot geve hir merci will admytt
The for gud will, that Is thy gyd and stere,
To quham for me thou pitousely requere.

196 And thus endith the fatall[2] Influeñce,
    Causit from hevyñ, quhare powar Is commytt
Of gouirnañce, by the magnificeñce
    Of him that hiest In the heviñ sitt;
    To quham we thank[3] that all oure [lif] hath writt,
Quho couth[4] It red, agone syne mony a ȝere,
'Hich In the hevyñnis figure circulere.'

197 Vnto [the] Impnis[5] of my maisteris dere,
    Gowere and chaucere, that oñ the steppis satt
Of rethorike, quhill thai were lyvand here,
    Superlatiue as poetis laureate
    In moralitee and eloqueñce ornate,
I recommend my buk In lynis sevin,
And eke thair saulis vn-to the blisse of heviñ.   Ameñ.

Explicit, &c. &c.

Quod Iacobus Primus, scotorum rex Illustrissimus.

---

[1] MS. salbe.   [2] MS. fotall.   [3] MS. think.
[4] MS. coutht.   [5] MS. Inpnis; *see* st. 33, l. 3.

GOOD COUNSEL

GOOD COUNSEL.

(EARLIEST VERSION.)

[*From MS. Camb. Kk.* 1. 5, *fol.* 5; *see Ratis Raving, ed. Lumby,* 1870, *p.* 10.]

SEN trew Vertew encressis dignytee,
    And wertew floure and rut is of noblay,
Of ony weill, of quhat esstat thow bee,
    His steppis sew,[1] and dreid the non affray :   4
    Exill all wyce,[2] and folow treuthe al-way ;
Luf most thi god, that fyrst thi lust began,
And for ilk ynch he wyll the quyte a spane.

[*The second stanza is missing.*]

Sen word is thrall, and thocht is only free,
    Thow dant thi twnge, that powar has and[3] may.   16
Thow set thine eene[4] fra worldly vanitee,
    Restren thi lust, and harkyne quhat I say.
    Stramp or thou slyd, and crep furth one the way ;
Kep thi behest one-to thi lord, and thane   20
Fore ilk ynch he will the quyt a spane.

---

[1] *So in* MS.; *misprinted* Ris steppis few.
[2] *Printed* wyte.   [3] MS. &; *misprinted* so.
[4] MS. erne (?); *printed* orne, *but the first letter is not* o.

(SECOND VERSION.)

[*From the Bannatyne MS., Edinburgh; fol.* 58, *back;* A.D. 1568.]

SEN throw vertew incressis dignitie,
    And vertew is floure and rute of nobill-ray,
Off ony vertewis estait that evir thow be,
    His steppis persew, and dreid the non effray.   4
    Exyle all vyce, and follow trewith alway ;
Luve most thy God that first thy luve began,
And for ilk inche he will the quyt a span.

Be not our prowde of thy prosperitie,   8
    For as it cumis, so will it pass away ;
Thy tyme to compt is schort, thow ma weill se,
    For of grene gress sone cumis wallowit hay.
    Labor in trewth, quhill licht is of the day ;   12
Trust most in God, for he best help the can,
And for ilk inche he will the quyt a span.

Sen wordis are thrall, and thocht is only fre,
    Thow dant thy tung that power hes and may ;   16
Thow steik thyne ene fra warldis vanitie ;
    Refrene thy lust ; harkin quhat I say ;
    Graip or thow slyd, and creip furth on the way,
And keip thy faith thow aw to God and man,   20
And for ilk inche he will the quyt a span.

          FINIS.

(THIRD VERSION.)

[*From "The Gude and Godlie Ballates,"* 1578, *repr.* 1868, *p.* 202. *Cf.*
Dalyell's Scotish Poems of the xvith *Cent., vol.* ii. *p.* 216.]

S EN throw Vertew incressis dignitie,
And vertew is flour and rute of Noblesse ay,
Of ony wit, or quhat estait thow be,
    His steppis follow, and dreid for none effray: 4
    Eject vice, and follow treuth alway:
Lufe maist thy God that first thy lufe began,
And for ilk inche he will the quyte ane span.

Be not ouir proude in thy prosperitie,   8
    For as it cummis, sa will it pas away;
The tyme to compt is schort, thow may weill se,
    For of grene gress sone cummis wallowit hay.
    Labour in treuth, quhilk suith is of thy fay;   12
Traist maist in God, for he best gyde the can,
And for ilk inche he will the quyte ane span.

Sen word is thrall, and thocht is only fre,
    Thou dant thy toung, that power hes and may,   16
Thou steik thy ene fra warldis vanitie:
    Refraine thy lust, and harkin quhat I say:
    Graip or thow slyde, and keip furth the hie way,
Thow hald the fast upon thy God and man,   20
And for ilk inche he will the quyte ane span.

Quod King James the First.

In Irving's 'Hist. of Scot. Poetry,' 1861, p. 152, a copy of the same poem
is printed from 'Ane Compentiovs Booke of godly and spiritvall Songs, newlie
corrected and amended by the first originall Copie': Edinb. 1621, 8vo. It
agrees with the above copy word for word, and the variations in spelling are
very slight. The chief of these are as follows: Line 1, vertue; 2, flowre,
nobles; 3, what estate; 4, steps; 7, thee; 10, well; 11, wallowed; 13, guide;
16, daunt; 17, eene; 18, harken what; 19, keep.

(RESTORED VERSION.)

[Founded upon collation of the preceding.]

SEN throu vertew encressis dignite,
    And vertew flour and rut is of noblay,
Of ony weill or quhat estat thou be,
    His steppis sew, and dreid thee non effray: 4
    Exil al vice, and folow trewth alway:
Luf maist thy God, that first thy luf began,
And for ilk inch he wil thee quyt a span.

Be not our proud in thy prosperite,   8
    For as it cumis, sa wil it pas away;
Thy tym to compt is schort, thou may weill se,
    For of green gres soyn cumis walowit hay.
    Labour in trewth, quhill licht is of the day.   12
Trust maist in God, for he best gyd thee can,
And for ilk inch he wil thee quyt a span.

Sen word is thrall, and thocht is only fre,
    Thou dant thy tung, that power hes and may;   16
Thou steik thyn een fra warldis vanite;
    Refrein thy lust, and harkin quhat I say;
    Graip or thou slyd, and creip furth on the way;
Keip thy behest unto thy God and man,   20
And for ilk inch he wil thee quyt a span.

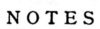

NOTES

*** THE following Notes are intended to explain peculiarities of construction, and to illustrate some of the allusions and expressions in the Poem. For the explanation of difficult *words*, recourse should be had to the Glossarial Index.

*** The references to 'Chaucer' are to the one-volume reprint of Chaucer's Works by Moxon, 1843, 8vo, an edition which contains Tyrwhitt's notes and glossary. In some instances I have rectified the spelling, so as to bring it nearer to the spelling used by the best scribes of the latter part of the fourteenth century.

NOTES.

TITLE. *Quair*, book; mod. E. *quire.* The word is used by Lydgate, in Lenvoye to the Black Knight :—

> Go, litel *quair*, unto my liues queen.

For the probable date of the Poem, see the Preface.

1. The first line of this stanza recurs in st. 196. See notes to that stanza.

Twynklyng; apparently a present participle, used as a nominative without a verb. Thus the sense is : *When* the ruddy stars *were* twinkling like fire, high in the circular figure (*i.e.,* dome) of the heavens. Otherwise, it is an error for *twinklen,* pl. of the pres. indicative. On the curious grammatical confusions so frequent in this Poem, see the Preface. In scanning the line, remember that *sterres* is dissyllabic; see the discussion of the metre in the Preface.

Aquary, the sign of Aquarius.

Citherea; an error of the scribe for *Cinthia, i.e.,* Cynthia, the moon. It was probably written *Cithia,* with a mark of contraction over the former *i,* and was then wrongly expanded. In the notes to st. 19 below, it is shown that the author himself sometimes confuses proper names; but he is not likely to have done so in this case, because we have the form *Synthius, i.e.,* Cynthius, applied to the sun in st. 20. Moreover, the scansion requires *Cinthia;* for the line will not scan well as it stands.[1] And see below.

Rynsid hir tressis, rinsed or cleansed her tresses, which resembled golden wire. The curious expression *rinsed* seems to be used with a poetical reference to the water-bearer Aquarius. Golden hair is frequently alluded to by Chaucer. According to him, Virginia's hair was golden—

> And Phebus dyed hath hire tresses grete
> Like to the stremes of his burned hete ; *C. T.* 11971.

---

[1] Still *Cithera* occurs in Chaucer; Troil. v. 1018. But then, so also does *Cinthia;* Troil. iv. 1608.

So was Creseide's—

> Hir ounded heer, that sonnish was of hewe;

i.e., her waved hair, of hue like the sun; Tro. and Cres. iv. 736.
So was Fame's—

> Her heer, that oundy was and crips [crisp]
> As burned gold it shoon to se; Ho. of Fame, iii. 296.

And so was that of the Duchess—

> For euery heer on her heed . . .
> Me thoughte most like gold it was; Book of the Duch. 855.

Through capricorn, &c.; heaved her bright horns through Capricorn. The moon had just passed out of Capricorn into Aquarius. The allusion to these 'horns' proves that the poet was thinking rather of the moon (Cynthia) than of Venus (Citherea). He was also doubtless thinking of Chaucer's lines here following :—

> The bente Mone with her hornes pale; Troil. iii. 624.

> I saw thin hornes olde eek by that morowe; id. v. 653.

The fact that Venus exhibits phases was not known till long after James's time, as Tytler well remarks.

Northward should probably be *northeward*, pronounced as a trisyllable. Otherwise, the line is defective.

Mydnyght, the meridian. A part of the meridian, as marked on an astrolabe, was called 'the north lyne, or elles the lyne of midnyght'; Chaucer, On the Astrolabe, pt. i. § 4.

2. *Quhen as* may either mean 'When, as' or 'When that'; as the reader is pleased to take it. Cf. st. 26, l. 1.

New partit, just departed, *i.e.*, just aroused or awaked.

A lyte, a little. Written *alyte* here in the MS., but as two words in stanza 53.

Fell me to mynd, there came to my mind, occurred to me; lit. it fell to me, to my mind, *me* being the dative case. See st. 10; cf. st. 11, last line.

For craft in erth, for (any) skill upon earth, for any earthly reason. It merely means 'by no manner of means.'

As tho, as at that time, on that occasion.

Toke a boke, took up a book. Compare the parallel passage in the opening lines of Chaucer's Book of the Duchess, where Chaucer tells us that he tried 'to drive the night away' by reading.

3. *Boece;* Boethius, the famous senator of Rome, and author of the favourite book of the middle ages, entitled De Consolatione Philosophiæ. King James might have read it in Chaucer's translation,[1] but he implies, in st. 7, that he read it in the Latin original. Several expressions in the King's Quair may be traced to Boethius, or to Chaucer's borrowings from Boethius, as noted below. Irving

---

1 See notes to st. 100.

remarks that "Boethius, who flourished during the iron age of Roman literature, has enjoyed a more extensive reputation than most of those who belonged to its age of gold. His book De Consolatione Philosophiæ was translated into Anglo-Saxon by King Alfred; it was translated into English by Chaucer, and more recently by Lord Preston, Mr Ridpath, and Mr Duncan. Another version appears to have been executed by a George Douglas: Hume of Godscroft has addressed a poem, 'Ad Georgium Duglasium, traducto Boethio de Consolatione.' See Lusus Poetici, p. 62; London, 1605, 4to." For further information, see the Preface to Chaucer's translation of Boethius, as edited by Dr Morris.

Schewing [the] counsele. In many places, I have found myself compelled to insert words which are necessary both to the sense and metre. These are distinguished, as here, by being enclosed within square brackets.

Quhilom, &c.; who was once upon a time the flower of the world.

Foriugit; was condemned by Fortune, for a time, to exile in poverty, (after being degraded) from his (former) high estate. *Foriugit, i.e.,* condemned, occurs in Lydgate's Poem of the Black Knight, l. 274, where we find :—

> Falsly accused, and of his foon [foes] *foriuged*
> Without answer, whil he was absent,
> He damned was, &c.

Mätzner gives no instance of its use; but it is precisely the F. *forjuger* (see the Glossary). It should be noted that Tytler unluckily printed the word as *foringit,* a mistake in which every editor has hitherto followed him; and to make the matter worse, this unmeaning and impossible form was admitted, on Tytler's authority, into Jamieson's great Dictionary.

4. *And there to here;* and (in reading the book, I) there (seemed) to hear, &c. The sense is clear, but it is almost impossible to parse the sentence. The poem abounds in similar awkward and incomplete constructions, which the reader must understand as he can.

Set a-werk, set a-work, set to work. Here *a* is for *an,* the same as the prep. *on.* Cf. *a-foot, a-sleep,* &c.

In his poetly report, in his poetic relation. The word *his,* which is hardly needed for the sense, is much in the way of the metre, and might advantageously be omitted. It is remarkable that Tytler here prints $\phi oetly$ (with a Greek ϕ) with the remark that "this is exactly copied from the MS." I see no real difference between the p in this word and in other places.

Can him to confort; at first sight, this seems to mean 'knows how to comfort himself.' But *can* is sometimes used as equivalent to *gan,* which our author uses both with *to* (st. 8, l. 2) and without it (st. 10, l. 6); see note to st. 10. Thus it means 'comforted himself.'

5. The construction is vague and unmeaning, though the general sense is clear. Perhaps *thoght* is to be explained as 'though'; but even then we cannot reduce the sentence to true order. The poet had intended to read merely to induce sleep, but soon discovered that his book was worthy of being carefully studied. Hence he says— " Wherefore, though I began with the purpose of borrowing sleep at that time from my book, ere I ceased, (I thought) my best (course) was to look more (closely) upon the writing of this noble man." If this construction be admitted, it would be better to replace the semi-colon at the end of the second line by a comma.

6. *Fortune*, &c.; Fortune turned her back to him.

Theire, their, makes no good sense; I propose to read *thir*, *i.e.*, those. See *Thir* in the Glossary.

Aworth he takith, he receives kindly; lit. at its worth. This resembles Chaucer's *receive in gre*, C. T. 4679, 9027.

7. *Rethorikly pykit*, rhetorically chosen (Tytler).

My scole, my skull, my head. Tytler explains it by 'my learning,' *i.e.*, lit. my school. This is very forced; no one speaks of his school, or even of his learning, as being 'too young.'

Leue all Incidence, omit all incidental matter, leave all digressions.

8. *Newe*, newly, freshly. The final *e* denotes the adverb, as in Chaucer's Clerkes Prol. l. 3.

Seyne should perhaps be *seyen;* but, in any case, it is here used as if dissyllabic. *To* requires the gerundial form, which frequently ends in -*e*, and always ended in -*ne* in Anglo-Saxon.

Thame translate, change themselves, *i.e.*, be changed.

9. *Tolter*, tottering; see the Glossary. It is merely the old form of *totter*, and is still in use even in provincial English, as shown in my Etym. Dict. s. v. *totter*. For a further description of Fortune's wheel, see st. 159, and 163-165. Cf. Chaucer, Troil. iii. 617:—

> But O Fortune, executrice of *werdis!*

Failyng foting, since they fail (to make good their) footing.

Quhen hir lest rele, when it pleases her to roll the wheel round.

10. *Gan oure-hayle*, recalled, reviewed, reconsidered. *Gan* is commonly a mere auxiliary, like our modern *did;* so that *gan love* would be merely a past tense, meaning no more than 'loved.' *Ouer-hayle* is exactly and curiously retained in the mod. E. *overhaul*, to reconsider, handle again, closely inspect. He recalls his past life.

Ne myght I nat, I could not; a double negative, as is common. For *myght* in the sense of 'could,' see st. 2, l. 5.

11. *For-wakit*, tired out with being awake. The curious use of these past participles should be noticed; it is the common idiom of the period. It would be quite wrong to suppose *forlyin* in the next line (which, by the way, is written in *one* word without any space after the prefix) to be equivalent to the modern *for lyin'*, *i.e.*, *for lying*, on account of lying. The idioms are totally distinct. *Forlyin* accurately represents the A.S. pp. *forligen*, just as *lien* in our Prayer-Book

Version of the Psalms accurately represents the A.S. p.p. *ligen.* I subjoin two instances of the same idiom in Chaucer. We find *Wery forwaked*, weary and tired of being awake; C. T. 5016. *Al horse forshright*, all hoarse, tired of shrieking; Troil. iv. 1147; where it is misprinted *for shright* (as two words) in Moxon's edition. In the Romaunt of the Rose, l. 3336, we find :—

> Forwery, *forwandred* as a fole ;

i.e., very weary, tired out with wandering about like a fool. And again, in P. Plowman, B. prol. 7, we find :—

> I was *wery forwandred*, and wente me to reste.

Compare also the p.p. *for-tirit*, tired out, occurring in st. 30 below. Also *despeired*, filled with despair, in the same; and *for-wepit*, *for-pleynit* in st. 73. *For-walowit* means 'tired out with tumbling from side to side in bed.' See the use of *wallow* in the Romaunt of the Rose, 2562; Chaucer's Legend of Good Women, 1164; Cant. Tales, 6667, 6684. In Chaucer, Troil. i. 699, Pandarus tells Troilus not 'to *wallow* and wepe.' Jamieson wrongly explains it by 'greatly withered.'

12. *Lyf*, living person; see the Glossary. This use of the word is common in P. Plowman and in Gower.

Dooth me think, makes me think.

13. *Made a cross.* The form of a cross was often prefixed to writings. The most notable instance is that of the horn-book, or alphabet for teaching children, which began with a cross, called the *Criss-cross*, *i.e.*, Christ's cross; in consequence of which the alphabet itself was termed the *Criss-cross-row*, or simply the *cross-row*, as in Shak. Rich. III., i. 1. 55.

14. *Wepe and waille*, an alliterative phrase; so Chaucer has "*wepe*, and wring, and *waille;*" C. T. 9088. Tytler compares the well-known passage from Pope's Essay on Man (pt. i. l. 77), beginning—"Heav'n from all creatures hides the book of fate."

15. *Stant*, contracted form for *standeth.* So also *abit* for *abideth;* see the Glossary.

Wantis It, lackest that which should rule and guide thee.

Ryght as, just as the ship that sails without a rudder must hasten to dangers upon the rocks, for lack of that which should be her aid. Imitated from Chaucer, Troil. bk. i. l. 416 :—

> Al stereles within a bote am I.

16. *By my-self*, with reference to myself, as in st. 70. *As in partye*, as in part, to some extent.

Suffisance, sufficiency, sufficient rank and honour; because he was born the second son of King Robert the Third.

Lakit; the pt. tense is evidently required. It means, nevertheless I lacked the ripeness of reason; because he was very young.

To gouerne with my will, to govern my will with. We now separate *with* from the verb; but in our old authors *with* and the verb are always close together; see *With* in the Glossary. This curious idiom has puzzled many. Chaucer again uses *stereles*, C. T. 4859; and, not long after, *driving*, id. 5367, 5389.

And how the case, and how the case stood.

17. *The wynd suld blowe*, the wind that should blow. This suppression of the relative is extremely common, and is often puzzling.

18. This stanza and part of the next are obviously imitated from the Proem to the second book of Chaucer's Troilus :—

> Out of these blake wawes let us saile,
> O winde, now the wether ginneth clere ;
> For in the se the bote hath such travaile,
> Of my conning that unnethe I it stere :
> This see clepe I the tempestous matere
> Of depe dispaire, that Troilus was inne ;
> But now of hope the calendes beginne.
>   O lady myn, that called art Cleo,
> Thou be my speed fro this forth, and my Muse,
> To rime wel this book til I haue do ; &c.

Chaucer has the word *prolixitee*, C. T. 10719.

19. *Cleo*, Clio; he uses the same spelling as occurs in the quotation just above.

Polymye, Polyhymnia. Proper names often appear in strange forms in our old writers. The parallel passage is in st. 3 of Chaucer's Annelida and Arcite.

> Be fauorable eek thou, *Polimnia*,
> On Pernaso that hast thy sisters glade.

Thesiphone, Tisiphone. Our author was doubtless misled by Chaucer, who invokes Tisiphone in the very first stanza of his Troilus, thus :—

> Thou Thesiphone, thou help me for tendite
> These woful vers, that wepen as I write.

Chaucer knew very well that Tisiphone was one of the furies; for he invokes "Megera, Alecto, and eek Tesiphonee" in the Proem to his Troilus, book iv. But King James does not seem to have remembered this, and doubtless assumed that Chaucer, in beginning his Troilus, must have invoked a Muse. The blunder is not one made by the scribe, as Tytler supposes, but by the author. Hence the critics are wrong in proposing to read *Terpsichore;* and most of all is Chalmers to blame, who coolly substitutes *Terpsichore* in the text itself, without a word of comment, or *any hint as to the MS. reading!* It need not be added that Chalmers's edition is, by a long way, the worst of all.

In nowmer ix, nine in number. Compare Chaucer, Troil. iii. 1810—

> Ye sustren nine eek, that by Helicone,
> In hill Pernaso, listen for tabide.

In this processe; guide my wayward wits in this undertaking.

20. *In vere*, in spring. The poets are very fond of this form of beginning. Compare the beginning of Chaucer's Prologue.

Synthius, Cynthius, the sun.

A morow, in the morning.

Vpward his course; to drive his course upward in the sign of Aries. By *upward* is meant Northward. The path of the sun crosses the equatorial line at the vernal equinox, and then proceeds northward, passing through the sign of Aries first. In Chaucer's time, as shown by his treatise On the Astrolabe, the vernal equinox was on the 12th of March. Consequently, King James is speaking of that day or of some day nearly succeeding it. Compare notes to st. 191.

In ariete, in Aries. We have here the Latin phrase, the prep. *in* being followed by the ablative case. But *Ariete* was also used for the accus. *Arietem*, and hence as a general form for *Aries*. This appears by the following phrase—viz., "out of this *Ariete*," Chaucer, Troil. iv. 1592; and again, id. v. 1190.

21. *Foure greis evin*, four degrees exactly, just four degrees. In the Squieres Tale, Part ii., Chaucer speaks of the sun being advanced four degrees in the Ram, and being also four degrees above the horizon. In the latter case, as also in our text, four degrees are equivalent to an hour. Our author is therefore speaking of an hour past mid-day, *i.e.*, one o'clock P.M.

Off lenth and brede . . . bryght, bright in their length and in their breadth, *i.e.*, wholly bright.

22. *Noght fer;* not far past the state of Innocence, but nearly about the number of three years (past it). The state of Innocence certainly means the age from birth to *seven* years, which was the period of infancy; the next age being that of childhood, from seven years to fourteen.

> Thus at vij 3eer age childhood bigynnes
> And folowith folies many-foold ;
> Aftirward his childhode blynnes,
> Whan he is fourtene 3eer olde.
> *The Mirror of the Period of Man's Life.*

See Hymns to the Virgin, ed. Furnivall, p. 60. See also Ratis Raving, ed. Lumby, p. 57, where the first age ends at three years, and the second at *seven*.

Tytler, without assigning any reason, pitched upon *nine* years as the age here meant, which, added to three, gives *twelve*, and contradicts the facts. By adding three to seven we get *ten;* and, as James was born in July 1394, we are thus brought to the year 1404; and it was on the 12th of April 1405, that he was taken prisoner by the English off Flamborough Head. The correction of Tytler's calculation was first made in Irving's Hist. of Scotish Poetry, which may well be consulted.

Were It causit, whether it were caused. The phrase *tak his auenture* occurs in Chaucer, C. T. 1188 ; cf. his Complaint of Mars, st. 3.

23. *Puruait of*, provided with all that was necessary for us. King

Robert, his father, determined to send him to France; but the ship was taken by the English, according to James's own account in st. 24, and the prince was confined as a prisoner in the Tower of London. "In 1407 he was removed to the castle of Nottingham; in 1413 we again find him in his former prison; and during the same year he was conducted to the castle of Windsor" (Irving).

Vp airly by the morowe, up early in the morning; cf. Chaucer, C. T. 16965. Chaucer has : *no longer wold* he *tary;* id. 12785.

The tyme I tald to-forowe, at the time, or date, which I told you before. This alludes to st. 20, where, as has been shown, he alludes to the 12th of March. As he was taken prisoner on the 12th of April, he is here referring to the time of his embarkation. How the month's interval can be accounted for is not clear. But some time was lost by the prince's temporary sojourn in the castle on the Bass Rock.

With mony fare wele; with many a farewell and many an exclamation of 'St John be your protection' from companion and friend.

Sanct Iohne to borowe, lit. 'St John for a protection,' or, 'for a protector.' *Borowe* is the dat. case of the sb. *borow*, a pledge, surety, not a verb. But of course the sense is equivalent to 'may St John protect you.' This was a favourite phrase as a farewell wish. Thus in Chaucer, Complaint of Mars, st. 2, we find :—

> Taketh your leue ; and, *with saint John to borowe*, &c.

And again, in the Cant. Tales, l. 10909 :—

> And toke him by the hond, *saint John to borowe*.

Irving, in his Hist. of Scot. Poetry, has a note on the phrase, showing that it occurs also in Blind Harry's Wallace, p. 224; Colkelbie's Sow, v. 648; Henryson's Fables, Edinb. 1621, p. 19; and Lindsay's Works, vol. i. p. 242.

Off falowe and frende, i.e., from companion and friend.

24. *Weltering*, (while we were) tossing about. Here again we have a present participle used instead of a verb.

Maugre, in spite of our wills. The poet adds—'to speak plainly, whether we would or not'; thus explaining the expression.

Off Inymyis, by enemies—viz., by the English.

Fortune It schupe, fortune provided that it should not be otherwise.

25. *Quhare as*, where that.

The secund sistere, the second of the three sisters (Fates) has taken heed to twine the unfortunate thread of my life. *Lukit* means lit. looked, hence, taken heed, given attention. The second sister, or Fate, was Lachesis, who spun out the thread of life; see Ovid, Trist. v. 10. 45; Spenser, F. Q., iv. 2. 48. Chaucer, in his Troilus, bk. v. st. 1, alludes to the "angry Parcas, sustren thre"; and again, in the same, bk. iii. l. 733, exclaims :—

> O fatal sustren, which, or any cloth
> Me shapen was, my destine me sponne.

Twise nyne; read *twies nine,* twice nine. By adding 18 to 10, we find that the poet is now speaking of himself at the age of 28. And again, by adding 18 to 1405, the year of his captivity, we obtain 1423; or, by adding 28 to 1394, the year of his birth, we obtain 1422; the slight discrepancy being due to a want of precise exactness as to the month intended. We can, however, settle this matter; for in st. 20, he is alluding to March 1405; and in stanzas 34, 49, and 65, he expressly mentions the month of May. This shows that the exact time here meant is May 1423; and we may further conclude that his Quair was written very soon afterwards, probably in May and June of the same year. This suits exactly with the date of his marriage, which took place on the 2d of February 1424.

Till Iupiter, till Jupiter was pleased to direct his mercy (towards me), and to send me comfort, by relaxing my sorrow.

26. *Quhare as,* where that, in my prison.

Quhat haue I gilt, in what have I offended, what sin have I committed? *Gilt* is the pp.

27. *Lakkith,* lack. This is a very curious instance of confusion of grammar; and it is hard to say whether it is due to the scribe, or to the poet's inexact imitation of Southern grammar. The form *lakkis* is equally suitable, in Northern English, for the *first* or for the *third* person; but *lakkith* in Southern English can only represent the *third* person. Here we have *lakkith* put for *lakkis,* and used with the first personal pronoun. The sense is 'and I lack.' See notes to st. 117, where a similar error is noted.

My folk I wold argewe, I would reason with my attendants. The chief of these was his tutor, Henry St Clair, Earl of Orkney; see Irving and Tytler.

28. *Me more comprisit,* included me rather than others. Tytler reads *more me comprisit;* but makes no comment on the fact that the word *me* has to be supplied; for it is not in the MS. Compare the first line of the stanza.

I suffer allone amang the figuris nyne, I alone suffer, among all the nine figures or numbers; or, as Tytler says, "of all the nine numbers, mine is the most unlucky or wretched." But neither he, nor any other editor, has made any attempt to explain the poet's meaning, nor do they make any comment on the two lines following. The clue is to be found in the fact that the poet is comparing himself to a cipher or O, which, though not strictly one of the *nine* Arabic numerals, is used conjointly with them. The peculiarity of the cipher is that it is of no use or value when standing *by itself,* but it has need of some one of the other figures before it can be rendered significant. When this idea is once caught, the passage is transparently clear. " I suffer when alone, being like a cipher amongst the other nine figures; I am like a wretched creature that can do no good to another (being intrinsically insignificant); and yet, on the other hand, I have

E

need of every person's (*i.e.*, figure's) help to support me and make me
of value." The phrase "like a cipher in augrim," *i.e.*, like a cipher
in arithmetic, seems to have been a proverbial expression for a worthless person. It is introduced, with a keenly satirical effect, in Rich-
ard the Redeles, iv. 53, where the author compares certain members
of Parliament to a "siphre in awgrym, that noteth a place, and
no-thing availith," *i.e.*, a cipher in arithmetic, which merely fills up
a place, but is of no intrinsic value. So also in Crowley's 'Select
Works,' ed. J. M. Cowper, p. 73:—

> And at the last thou shalt be founde
> To occupye a place only
> As do in A[u]g[r]ime ziphres rounde; &c.

Chaucer speaks of the "figures ten"; Book of the Duchess, l. 437.

29. *For quhich*, on which account, in order to seek for comfort as a
remedy for my distress.

By the come I, by thee I came. *Thee* refers to *exercise* or habit;
and *come* is the past tense.

30. The description here given is a palpable imitation of Chaucer's
Knightes Tale, where it is recorded how Palamon and Arcite, being in
prison, first saw Emelie walking in the garden. The first line of the
stanza is borrowed exactly, with the mere change of *his* to *my*, from
Chaucer, Troil. bk. i. l. 547, where it is spoken of Troilus.

31. Compare Chaucer, C. T. 1058:—

> The grete tour, that was so thikke and strong . . .
> Was euen Ioinaunt to the garden-wall,
> Ther as this Emelye had hire pleying.

But the poet had also here some remembrance of Chaucer's
Assembly of Foules, where there is a description of "a garden . . .
full of blossomed bowis," with "trees clad with leues," &c. This is
made certain by the closer imitation of the same passage in stanzas
152, 153.

Herbere, a place for growing shrubs and trees; from O. F. *herbere*,
Lat. *herbarium*. By the description here given, we find that it contained alleys, was railed round, and was set round with trees and
hawthorn-hedges. In the next stanza, the same word *herbere* is
used to denote the smaller beds into which the *herbarium* was sub-
divided; each bed containing juniper-trees, so closely placed to one
another that, to a person who only saw the garden from a distance,
the trees seemed almost to fill up the beds. Observe also the use of
lyf for 'person' both in st. 31 and st. 32. Chaucer mentions *An
herber grene;* Troil. ii. 1705. The place described is the royal garden
at Windsor.

33. Here again we see some imitation of Chaucer's Assembly of
Foules, l. 190:—

> On euery bough the birdes herde I singe.

And in l. 684 of the same, we find:—

> Thus singen smale foules for thy sake,

i.e., for the sake of St Valentine, or the pairing season.
Again, in Chaucer's Troil. bk. ii. l. 918 :—

> A nightingale upon a cedre grene . . .
> Full loude song ayen the mone shene,
> Paraunture, in his birdes wise, a lay
> Of loue, &c.

But the whole of stanzas 33 and 34 are clearly founded upon the
stanzas last but two and last but one of the Assembly of Foules,
which contain such lines as these :—

> But first were chosen foules for to singe . . .
> To do Nature honour and plesaunce ;
> The note, I trowe, maked was in Fraunce,
> The wordes were such as ye may here fynde
> The nexte vers, as I now haue in mynde :
> *Qui bien ayme, tard oublye.*
> ' Now welcome somer, with thy sunnes softe
> That hast this winter wethers ouershake :
> Saint Valentine, thou art ful high on-lofte,
> Which driuest away the longe nightes blake ; '
> Thus singen smale foules for thy sake,
> Wel haue they cause for to gladden ofte,
> Sens eche of hem recouered hath his make; &c.

Rong, rung entirely with their song. Hence we should probably
read *of* for *on* before *the copill*, and explain it by—'and with the
couple (*i.e.*, verse or stanza) next following, containing their sweet
harmony ; and behold, here is the text of it.'

34. *Worschippe*, a trisyllabic form. Probably the poet used
Chaucer's usual form *worschippeth ;* the termination *-eth* being that
of the imperative plural in the Southern dialect.

The kalendis, the calends are begun. The birds are here described
as welcoming the calends or first days of bliss. So also, in st. 177,
the author speaks of the *kalendis of confort.* This expression is imitated from Chaucer, who speaks of the *kalendes of hope*, Troil. ii. 7,
and of the *kalends of eschaunge*, id. v. 1646. In the first line, lovers
are exhorted to pay respect to May, with reference to the usual poetical invocation of the springtime of love; and it is even possible that
kalendis may be meant in the literal sense, with reference to the *first*
of that month, and the rejoicings commonly connected with it. May
is mentioned again in stanzas 49 and 65.

Hevynnis wonne, won your heavens, *i.e.*, your states of bliss. It is
synonymous with *makis wonne*, won their mates, in the next stanza.

Thank lufe, thank Love, who is pleased to call you to his mercy.

36. *Lyf*, mode of life ; not ' person,' as elsewhere.

37. *Eft*, again. The idea is more or less copied from Chaucer, C. T. 1171, &c. :—

> A man most nedes loue, maugre his heed.

Compare also 'the Song of Troilus,' in Chaucer, Troil. bk. i.

38. Cf. Who hath thee *doon offence ?* Ch. C. T. 1085.

40. Imitated from Chaucer, C. T. 1079 :—

> He cast his eyen vpon Emilia ;

Also from l. 1063 :—

> Ther as Emilia had hire pleying;

And from ll. 1037-9 :—

> That Emelie, that fayrer was to sene
> Than is the lilie vpon hire stalke grene,
> And fressher than the May with floures newe.

And further, compare ll. 1080, 1081 :—

> And therwithal he blente, and cried a !
> As though he stongen were vnto the herte.

Pleyne is for *pleyn*, *i.e.*, play, amuse herself. It is Chaucer's very word, and Tytler is quite wrong in supposing it to mean 'complain' in this passage; though of course it often bears that meaning. In Chaucer's Troil. ii. 812, it is said of Cressid :—

> She rist her up, and wente her *for to pleye ;*

And, five lines below, *To pleyen.*

41. *For-quhy*, because, since.

Of free wyll, of my own free will ; for there was no token (or sign) of menace (or threatening) in her sweet face.

42. The last two lines are due to Chaucer, C. T. 1103 :—

> I not wher [*know not whether*] she be womman or goddesse.

And again, in Chaucer, Troil. i. 425:—

> But whether goddesse or womman, iwis,
> She be, I not [*know not*].

43. *Nature the goddesse.* Chaucer, in his Assembly of Foules, introduces Nature as a goddess, and assigns her a garden ; l. 302 :—

> And in a launde, vpon an hille of floures,
> Was set this noble goddesse Nature.

Minister. This is obviously the word meant, though written 'mister' in the MS. A trisyllabic word is required. Tytler wrongly prints *mester*, but suggests 'administer' as the sense of it.

E. Thomson (p. xiii.) notes another instance where the word *minister* is written as 'mister' in a MS.—viz., in the Acts of James I. 1432, c. 4, where we find : 'Jugis sal mister the law.'

44. *I may It noght astert*, I cannot escape it. Cf. Chaucer, C. T. 1595.

That dooth me sike, that causes me to sigh. Tytler did not understand this, though the construction is common enough.

Quhy lest, why did it please God to make you such as to cause a poor prisoner thus to suffer? One, namely, who entirely loves you, and knows only of wo.

45. *Vnknawin*, it being unknown to me. Such is the literal sense, *unknawin* being a past participle; but the present participle *vnknawing* would be simpler.

I-fallyng, on the other hand, certainly stands for *I-fallen*, fallen, pp. On the confusion between the suffixes *-ing* and *-en* in pieces written by Scottish writers in imitation of Southern English, see my Preface to Lancelot of the Laik, printed for the Early English Text Society; and see notes to st. 164.

Lufis dance, the dance of love. This curious expression occurs in Chaucer, C. T. 478; it is said of the Wife of Bath that she knew "the olde dance" of the art of love. It occurs again in C. T. 12013, and in Troil. bk. iii. l. 696. Tyrwhitt explains it by 'game,' and remarks that the French have the same phrase, citing from Cotgrave (s. v. *Danse*) the expression, 'Elle sçait assez de la vieille danse'; the translation of which is to be found in l. 4300 of the Romaunt of the Rose—'For she knew al the olde daunce.' See also st. 185, l. 2.

46. This description of the lady Joan should be compared with the description of Creseide in Chaucer's Troilus, bk. v. ll. 807-827.

Toward; I can only assign meaning to this passage by supposing that *toward* here means 'in front.' If this be not a legitimate use of the word, there must be something wrong in the text. We can hardly take it to mean 'regarding'; and even if we do, this line will not suit the next.

In fret-wise couchit was, was trimmed or set with a fretwork of pearls. *Couch*, F. *coucher*, is the Lat. *collocare*, and is here used with the sense of arranging or setting in order; hence, of trimming. The expression is copied from Chaucer, C. T. 2163 :—

> *Couched* with perles, white, and rounde, and grete.

And again :—

> A *fret* of gold she hadde next her heer ; Legend of Good Women, 215.

Off plumys. Compare Chaucer, C. T. 1055 :—

> She gadereth floures, party white and rede,
> To make a sotel gerlaund for her heede.

47. *Amorettis*, love-knots, according to Jamieson. The word is borrowed from Le Roman de la Rose, where it occurs twice. The English version of the Romaunt also employs the word, ll. 890 and 4755 :—

> For not y-clad in silk was he,
> But al in floures and flourettes,
> I-peinted al with *amorettes*,
> And with losenges and scochouns
> With birdes, liberdes, and liouns.

And again :—

> For also wel wol loue be set
> Under ragges as rich rochet ;
> And eek as wel by *amorettes*
> In mourning blake, as bright burnettes.

In the latter passage Tyrwhitt explains *amorette* by 'an amorous woman,' which seems quite right; Cotgrave quotes the very lines of *le Roman de la Rose* (4437, &c.) which are here cited. But it is obvious that the same explanation will not apply to the other passage, which Tyrwhitt omitted to note or observe ; whilst at the same time, this other passage is the very one of which King James was thinking. Cotgrave also assigns to the word the sense of 'love-trick'; but it is clearly here used in the sense of 'love-device' or 'love-ornament.' What was really the *precise shape* of the *amorette*, it would now be hard to say ; it can hardly have been precisely a knot or love-knot, as that would be an awkward shape, I fancy, for a spangle. It is perhaps worth adding that, according to Sigart, the Walloon word *amourette* is still used to mean penny-cress, the English name of which is due to 'the resemblance which its seed-vessels in size and shape bear to silver pennies'; Johns, Flowers of the Field, 4th ed. p. 40. Perhaps it is meant, accordingly, that the spangles were thin and circular, which is their usual shape.

Floure-Ionettis, flowers of the great St John's wort ; see the Glossary. The great St John's wort actually has, as it were, a tuft of stamens in the centre of the flower, which may most aptly be compared to a golden plume ; or, conversely, a golden plume may be compared to the tuft. This leaves no doubt as to the flower intended. Tytler supposes that the king "may have dubbed some flower with the name *janetta*, in honour of his mistress, the lady Jane." But the name *jaunette* is a real one, though it is quite possible that it was chosen with a punning reference to *Joan*, which better represents the name of the lady ; for it is spelt *Johanne* in the Chronicle of London quoted by Irving.

Round crokettis. These two words are inserted by me, merely to fill up the line ; it is obvious that the MS. is wrong in repeating *floure-Ionettis* from the line above. It is very difficult to find words that rime ; we have only the choice of *flourettis* (see the quotation from the Romaunt of the Rose just above), or *violettis*, or *crokettis*—unless there be some other word which has escaped me. The poet would hardly compare plumes to flowerets (little flowers) or to violets, just after comparing them to another flower ; but the comparison to *crockets* is just conceivable, though not perhaps highly appropriate. A crocket was a sort of curled tuft, and was actually used of a particular kind of ornament for the hair. Sir F. Madden, in his remarks on Havelok the Dane, shews that *Athelstan with the golden crocket* is the name of a lost romance ; see Havelok, ed. Skeat, p. vi. note 1. Indeed, the word still survives as a term of architecture. Still, if any critic can make a better guess, by all means let him do so.

48. Compare Chaucer's description of a lady's neck and throat in the Book of the Duchess, ll. 939-947.

Herte is properly a dissyllable in Chaucer.

Now gif, now God knows if there was a good partner (for me to choose). The line just expresses that which we could now only express by the vulgar phrase, that she was indeed 'an eligible party.' But if it be questionable English, it is excellent French. Cotgrave explains *parti* by 'a match, bargaine, . . . and hence a husband or wife'; &c.

49. See Chaucer, C. T. 1036, where he describes Emily as going out to walk 'ones, in a morwe of May.'

To suich delyte, to such (an extent of) delight, so delightful. Perhaps *of* would be better than *to* here.

50. These lines are a reminiscence of Chaucer, C. T. 4582 :—

> In hire is heigh beaute, withouten pride,
> Youthe, withouten grenehed or folye ;
> To alle hire werkes vertue is hire gyde ; &c.

This is his description of Constance.

51. Cf. Chaucer, C. T. 1161:—

> And myn is loue, as to a *creature.*

Thir versis sevin, these seven verses—*i.e.,* this stanza. See the stanza next following.

52. *Of goddis stellifyit,* made into a star (planet) by the gods. Chaucer talks of Jupiter 'stellifying' Alcestis; Legend of Good Women, 525. See also the House of Fame, bk. ii. l. 78.

In such a wise, in such a manner ; I have inserted *a* for the metre.

53. *Bellis,* bells fastened to the dog's collar.

A ! wele were him, Ah ! well would it be for him.

55. *Proigne,* Progne. Cf. Chaucer, Troil. ii. 64:—

> The swalwe Progne, with a sorowful lay
> Whan morow com, gan make hire waimenting
> Why she forshapen was.

See the whole story related at length in Chaucer's Legend of Philomene, which is the seventh story in his Legend of Good Women, and is taken from the sixth book of Ovid's Metamorphoses. Tereus married Progne; and, after ravishing her sister Philomela, whose tongue he cut out, he assured Progne that Philomela was dead. This tragedy was occasioned by Philomela's desire to see her sister; hence our poet exclaims: 'And eke I pray, for the sake of all the great pains that thou didst once suffer owing to thy love for thy dear sister Progne, at the time when thy breasts were wetted with the tears of thy bright eyes, (and were) all run over (or besmeared) with blood ; so that it was a pity to hear,' &c. Progne was turned into a swallow, and Philomela into a nightingale, as is here said. This James may

have borrowed from Gower, Conf. Amantis, bk. v. ed. Pauli, ii.
318 :—

> So what with blode, and what with teres
> Out of hir eyen and hir mouth,
> He made hir faire face vncouth.

56. *The treson*, the treacherous deed ; as in Ch. C. T. 2003.

Kythit, shewn. He shewed his treason by falsely asserting
Philomela's death. We need not take *kythit* in its literal sense of
' made known,' as this would contradict the story.

In the twenty deuil way, lit. in the way of twenty devils. This was an expression of impatience, meaning little more than ' by all possible means.'
Chaucer uses it in the form *a twenty deuil wey*, where *a* stands for *an*,
i.e., on or in. Examples occur in Cant. Tales, 3713, 4255, and 16250 ;
we also find *a deuil wey*, ll. 3136, 7824. Tytler was so puzzled by this
common expression that he supposed *deuil* to represent the F. *deuil*,
sorrow ! We may remark that it would improve the metre to substitute *a* (as in Chaucer) for *in the*.

57. *Hastow no lest*, hast thou no desire?

Say ones to me 'pepe,' say but once to me ' peep !' *Peep* is an imita-
tive word, allied to *pipe*, to express the chirping of a bird.

59. *Wyn gree*, win the victory. Tytler calls this ' a Scottish phrase,'
but we find *the gree* for the victory, or the prize, in Chaucer, C. T.
2735 ; and the phrase, ' The *gree* yit hath he geten' occurs in P. Plowman, B. xviii. 98.

60. *Cast*, *i.e.*, throw (a stone).

Hald me pes, hold my peace. Tytler substitutes *my* for *me* in the
text, without any hint that the MS. reading is *me*.

Do the leuis, make the leaves shake.

61. For *he* in l. 1, it would be better to read *sche*. Here again
Tytler inserts *sche* in the text, without any hint that the MS. has *he*.
But then he never saw the MS. himself. Compare l. 2 of the next
stanza.

Boundin all to fest, bound all too fast, *i.e.*, completely taken captive.
Tytler prints *bound in*, and then explains it by ' so were all my wits
(or senses) feasted' ; thus ignoring *boundin* (or *bound in*) altogether.

62. 'I there made a ditty, addressed to her who was my heart's
queen, (adapted) to the notes of the nightingale, which she (the bird)
sang.' *Philomene* is from the Low Lat. *philomena*, a substitution for
the Lat. *philomela*. For this form, see A. Neckam, De Naturis Rerum,
ed. Wright, pp. 102, 390 ; and see Chaucer's Legend of *Philomene*,
where this spelling occurs repeatedly.

63. *Is ȝit vncouth*, is as yet unknown. Tytler has no stop at the end
of l. 4, and Thomson proposes to consider *throu-folow* as one word,
which I do not think is admissible, and, after all, gives no sense. The
sense of this difficult stanza (unintelligible with the old punctuation)
I take to be as follows : " When will your mercy take pity upon your

lover, whose service is as yet unknown to you? Since, when you depart, there is nothing else (for me) then, except (to say): O heart, where that the body cannot (go) through, do thou (at least) follow thy heaven (*i.e.*, thy lady's person)! Who (my heart!) ought to be glad except thou, who hast undertaken to follow such a guide? Even were it through hell, refuse thou not the way."

To *forsake* is to refuse, shrink from.

64. *With a voce*, all with one voice; *a* is emphatic. So also three lines below, *a soyte* means one suit, one livery, one dress.

65. Here again we have an invocation to May, which is here mentioned for the third time; cf. notes to st. 34 and to st. 49.

Bridis, brides, spouses. There is some difficulty here, as we should rather have expected the reading *briddis*, *i.e.*, birds; but this is forbidden by the rime. We must clearly take *bydis* to mean 'bides' or 'abides,' and so cannot read *byddis*, *i.e.*, bids. Still May may be considered as the season of love, and so 'merciful to brides' as well as to birds. Compare the Cant. Tales, ll. 1502, 1503 :—

> And for to don his observance to *May*,
> Remembring *on the point of his desire*.

Observe also ll. 1512, 1513 :—

> O May, with alle thy floures and thy grene,
> Right welcome be thou, faire fresche May !

May is the name of the *bride herself* in Chaucer's Marchauntes Tale, to which James explicitly refers in st. 110. And we may compare Milton's Song on May Morning :—

> Hail bounteous May, that dost inspire
> Mirth, and youth, and warm desire.

66. *Facture*, feature, aspect. The MS. plainly has *facture*, both here and in st. 50; Tytler should not have altered it to *faiture*. Cf. O. F. *facture*, 'the facture, workmanship, framing, or making of a thing'; Cotgrave. The mod. E. *feature* represents Lat. *factura*, just as the O. F. *facture* does.

67. *A lytill thrawe*, a little while.

68. For *quhare-to* I propose to read *quhare-vnto*, as it improves the metre, and is somewhat better for the sense.

Of peyne; of pain? surely not; and yet, God knows, it *is* so; for they (such pains) cannot more strongly torment any one. Here *ȝa* means *yea*, *i.e.*, yet it is so. *Thay* agrees with a plural *peynes*, not expressed, but implied in the preceding singular *peyne*.

69. *Thrist*, thirst; misprinted *thirst* by Tytler. The form is common.

Bot venus, unless Venus, of her grace, will provide a remedy, or cause my spirit to pass hence, *i.e.*, cause me to die. He means, I must attain my desire, or die. Tytler explains it quite amiss by 'bring peace to, or calm my spirit.' But the old spelling of 'peace' is not *pace*, but *pees*. Cf. Chaucer, Cant. Tales, 8968:—

> No force of deth, ne when my spirit pace.

Again, in l. 10808:—

> Myn harm I wol confessen er I pace,

i.e., ere I die.
And again, in Troil. iv. 951:—

> To *doon* him sone out of the world *to pace.*

70. *Ay but-les*, for ever boot-less, for ever without success. Chaucer alludes to Tantalus; Troil. iii. 593.

Euer ylike, ever in the same way, always unchangingly.

By my-self, with reference to myself, as in st. 16.

71. *God mote hir conuoye*, may God accompany her on her way.

72. *This is to say*, this is as much as to say, the night approached. This humorous touch is precisely copied from Chaucer, C. T. 11329 :—

> For thorizont had reft the sonne his light ;
> This is as much to seyn, as it was night.

Chaucer has a similar touch of humour in his Troil. ii. 904:—

> The dayes honour, and the heuenes eye,
> The nightes foo—al this clepe I the sonne.

Esperus, Hesperus, the evening-star. Lydgate applies the term *Esperus* to the planet Venus; Complaint of the Black Knight, l. 612. But, by the epithet *his*, it would seem to be here applied to the planet Jupiter. Both planets have been called 'the evening-star.' Chaucer has the expression *as still as stoon;* C. T. 7997.

73. *For-wepit and for-pleynit*, tired out with weeping and complaining ; see note to st. 11.

Ourset so, sorrow had so overset (or overwhelmed) both my heart and mind. For *overset*, we now say *upset*.

Lent, leaned. Tytler alters it to *lenit*, unnecessarily and without authority. *Lened*, leant, occurs in P. Plowman, B. viii. 65 ; of which *lent* is a shorter form. And see st. 74, l. 2 ; st. 191, l. 2.

Suoun, in a swoon. But it is really quite right ; for *swoon* was orig. a pp., A.S. *swógen*. See *swoon* in my Etym. Dictionary.

Met, dreamt. *Deuise 3ou*, tell you.

74. *Of my sicht*, the power of my sight became wholly blind. Or we might take *Iblent* actively, the nom. *it* being understood ; 'the light wholly blinded the power of my sight.' The former seems to be here intended ; Chaucer has *blente*, blinded, in Troil. v. 1194.

75. *Nas nothing*, there was not anything against me, *i.e.*, to oppose my way. *Nas* is commonly used for *ne was*, was not. Tytler prints *was*, against the MS. reading.

Clippit, embraced. Compare the account in Chaucer's House of Fame, bk. i., where the poet describes his being carried through the air by an eagle.

76. *Spere*, sphere. The ancients supposed there were nine spheres, or as Chaucer calls them *nine speris;* Assembly of Foules, l. 59. See my edition of Chaucer's Astrolabie. They also supposed that the earth, the centre of all things, was surrounded by air, outside of which was a sphere (or shell) of water, and again a sphere of fire. Hence the poet ascends, successively, through air, water, and fire, till he comes to *Signifer*, or the ' sign-bearing' zodiac, containing the twelve signs. Finally, he arrives in the planet Venus. In the sixth line, I have supplied *quhar* (where) as being no less requisite for the sense than the metre. Chaucer has the word *Signifer ;* Troil. v. 1020. A long description of the elements, spheres, and signs is given by Gower; Conf. Amantis, bk. vii.

77. *Quhen as*, when that; a common phrase. I have supplied *as*, for the metre. Cf. *there as*, where that, in st. 86.

As quho sais, lit. as who says; as if one should say.

At a thoght, at a thought, as quick as one can think.

Grete repaire, a great resort, *i.e.*, a great concourse. Tytler observes that he takes the expressions *as quho sais at a thoght* and *of peple grete repaire* to be both Scottish. I do not see any reason for this. Chaucer has the following, in Troil. iii. 267:—

> For wel thou wost, the name as yet of her
> Amonges the peple, *as who saith*, halowed is.

And again, in the Book of the Duchess, l. 559 :—

> *As who saith*, nay, that nil not be.

And again, in his tr. of Boethius, bk. iii. pr. 4, ed. Morris, l. 2046 : 'as *who seith*, none.'

Chaucer also uses *repaire* in the very sense of great resort, or concourse of people ; C. T. 6806.

78. *Endit had*, had ended. The word *had*, here supplied, greatly improves both the sense and metre. *Endit had* occurs elsewhere, just above—viz., in st. 72, l. 2.

Chancis, adventures, histories.

Diuerse bukis, various books. Tytler supposes that the poet had ' the celebrated *Tablature of Cebes* in his view, although his groupes of figures are different.' It is much more likely that he was thinking of the stories in Ovid, and of Chaucer's allusion to them in the Man of Law's Prologue, which see. Compare also Chaucer's Legend of Good Women, and the description of lovers in Gower, Conf. Amantis, bk. viii. ed. Pauli, iii. 359.

79. *Martris and confessouris*, martyrs and confessors for love, just as the saints were such for Christ. This is quite in the medieval tone. Chaucer actually calls the Legend of Good Women his ' seintes legende of Cupide '; C. T. 4481.

His make in his hand, *i.e.*, holding his mate by the hand.

Solempnit, rendered solemn. The MS. has *solempt*, an impossible form, and too short by a syllable. Or we may read *solempne*, if we keep its trisyllabic form, as in Chaucer, C. T. 10425 :—

> My liegë lord, on this solempnë day.

After as lufe, according as Love is pleased to advance them.

80. *Off gude folkis*, some good folks. *That faire In lufe befill*, to whom it happened favourably in love. *That* is really a dat. plural here. *By thame one*, by themselves; a common idiom. Tytler actually seems to have taken *one* to mean an individual; for he explains it by 'Prudence with his hoary head,' evolving *Prudence* out of his own consciousness, as being a likely person to have a hoary head. But *hedis* is plural, and not even Prudence has more heads than one, as E. Thomson pertinently remarks. See st. 83, l. 4.

I subjoin a list of the various groups of lovers whom the poet mentions :—

1. Lovers with hoary heads; near them stood Good-will (st. 80).
2. Next them were young lovers, amongst whom was Courage (st. 80).
3. A group in wide capes, with hoods hanging over their eyes; amongst them stood Repentance (81).
4. Behind a traverse or thin screen stood 'a world of folk,' with discontented looks, holding in their hands *bills* or petitions containing their complaints (82).

In the stanzas next following, further explanatory remarks are made concerning these groups; hence we learn that the *first* group included the true lovers, constant even in their old age, and all who were true to Venus, both warriors and poets (83-85). The *second* group included the lovers who died young, from various causes (86, 87). The *third*, 'men of religion,' who hid their conduct from the world, but served Love in secret (88, 89). The *fourth* group consisted of the young folks who were not permitted to pursue their love, but were shut up by their friends in a cloister (90); or else they were married to those whom they could not love (91, 92); or died very shortly after being married happily (93).

82. *Trevesse*, a traverse, or transparent curtain; better spelt *trauerse* in st. 90, where it is called 'a traverse of delight,' *i.e.*, delightful to look upon. The third line of the stanza is imperfect; we seem to require the form *y-standing*.

84. *Of lufis craft the cure;* this is put in apposition with *exercise*, so that it means 'the exercise which is the cure of the craft of love,' *i.e.*, love-play or dalliance.

85. *Faucht*, who fought; the relative being omitted.

Mynd, memory, remembrance. Ovid's poems were probably better known in the middle ages than those of any other writer. Homer is not often mentioned, because the tale of Troy was learnt from Guido de Colonna's version. Still Chaucer's House of Fame contained

> the grete Omer,
> And with him Dares and Titus
> Before, and eek he Lollius,
> And Guido eek de Columpnis.

86. *Wanting,* lacking; not because they wanted or desired their mates, but because they could not get them.

87. *All day,* continually; see Chaucer, C. T. 1526.

Surmounting, aspiring above their rank.

89. *Halfdel cowardy,* in a half measure, cowardice. The MS. has merely *half,* but *halfdel* is the right phrase, and though composed of *half* and *del* (deal, part), is often written as one word.

90. *Take,* taken. *Nothing thay to wyte,* they (being) in no respect to blame.

Recounsilit, reconciled, *i.e.,* to their mates or lovers; restored to them.

On thame to pleyne, to complain against them.

91. *For he,* because he. For *gruch,* Sibbald actually substitutes the unmeaning word *bruckt. For quhich,* on which account.

92. *Coplit,* coupled with others that could not agree (with them).

Departing, separating those that would never have disagreed.

Fro thair chose dryve, driven from their choice; for *chose,* see the Glossary, or compare st. 147.

93. By reading *Sche* for *So* (in the MS.) in the fifth line, the sense of the stanza is at once obvious; with the old reading, it is nonsense. Perhaps the original had *Sho,* not an unusual form of *she.*

94. *Chiere,* chair. But it is ill spelt; it should rather be *chaiere.* Tytler well remarks that it is worth while to compare this description of the winged Cupid with Milton's splendid description of Raphael in the Paradise Lost, bk. v. 277. King James may have been thinking of Chaucer, C. T. 1965:—

> Before hire stood hire sone Cupido,
> Upon his shuldres winges had he two ;
> And blind he was, as it is often sene,
> A bowe he bar, and arwes brighte and kene.

And we may also observe the description in Chaucer's Legend of Good Women, l. 234:—

> And in his hond, me thoughte, I saw him holde
> Two fyry dartes, as the gledes rede,
> And angelike his winges saw I sprede ;
> And, al be that men sain that blind is he ; &c.

Thre arowis ; three arrows, of diverse metals—viz., one of gold, one of silver, and one of steel. I do not know whence King James derived these *three* arrows of Cupid. In the description just quoted, he has but *two* darts. In the Romaunt of the Rose, Love has *ten* arrows, which are particularly described. But the most likely source is Chaucer's Assembly of Foules, 211-217, where Cupid is said to have some arrows (the number of them not being mentioned), the heads of which his daughter tempers in a well, so

> as they should serve
> Some [for] to slee, and some to wounde and kerve.

Here we have the notion of the different effects produced by different arrows.

95. *A chaplet.* In the Romaunt of the Rose, Love is described as having a chaplet of red roses on his head.

96. *Depeyntit with sighis,* painted or ornamented with sighs. Imitated from Chaucer, C. T. 1920 :—

> First in the temple of Venus maistow see
> *Wrought* on the wall, ful pitous to beholde,
> The broken slepes, and the *sikes* colde.

Fond I venus, I found Venus. Imitated from Chaucer, Assembly of Foules, 260-273 :—

> And in a privy corner, in disport
> Fond I Venus, and her porter Richesse . . .
> And on a bedde of gold she lay to reste ; &c.

97. *Fair-calling.* In the Assembly of Foules, the porter of Venus is named *Richesse,* Riches ; in the Knightes Tale, he is named Idleness. The name of Fair-calling may have been suggested by the name *Belacoil, i.e.,* Fair-greeting, in the Romaunt of the Rose.

In l. 5 of this stanza, the word *that* should rather be omitted, that the line may run smoothly ; it may easily be understood.

98. *Salute,* saluted ; the past tense.

99. *By vertew pure,* by the pure virtue (or might) of your powerful aspects. *Virtue* often means power or effect, as in l. 4 of Chaucer's Prologue. In l. 6, *pure* means ' poor.' The poet alludes to the supposed power of the planet Venus in astrology.

100. *Of carefull hertes cure,* the cure of anxious hearts ; and, amid the huge fell rolling waves of love's rage, (art the) blissful and sure haven. Tytler says—' the huge rolling waves of Love's fell rage'; which makes *fell* agree with the wrong substantive. Still, he rightly saw that *fell* is here an adjective.

Anker and keye, anchor and guide (see below). Tytler misprints *treue* for *keye,* though it is plainly written, and strangely explains it by ' true anchor.' He does not pay much heed to grammatical construction. For *keye,* Sibbald strangely substitutes the meaningless word *trige!* As to the meaning of *keye,* we have the choice of *key* or *quay.* The latter would be quite in keeping, since James calls Venus *a haven* in the preceding line ; but I have no doubt that the sense is *key, i.e.,* helm or guide, for the following reason—viz., that Chaucer misled him. In Chaucer's tr. of Boethius, bk. iii. pr. 12 (l. 2926, ed. Morris), where the original has *clauus et gubernaculum* (*i.e.,* rudder and helm), we actually find the rendering ' a *keye* and a stiere'; where it is obvious that our great poet was thinking of *clavis,* a key. We also learn by this that King James had read Chaucer's translation as well as the original, but had not detected this particular error.

Man, servant; the usual term. So again in st. 187. So Troilus says of Creseide, in Chaucer's Troil. i. 427 :—

> But as *her man* I wol ay liue and sterue.

Cf. E. *homage*, as derived from F. *homme*.

102. *Do me steruen*, cause me to die, kill me instantly.

103. *Law*, low down, below me.

104. *Efter grace*, *i.e.*, to obtain grace. In l. 4, Tytler prints *She kest*, which alone will make sense; but he does not notice that the MS. really has the reading *Me kest*.

106. *Paciently* is here to be pronounced with *four* syllables; the line will then scan. *Pacience* is *three* syllables in st. 125, l. 2. The line is taken almost directly from Chaucer's Complaint of Mars, l. 21 :

> And patiently takth your auenture.

This will my son, this my son desires.

He can the stroke, he knows (how to deal) the stroke.

Humily, humbly. Quite a correct form; Tytler actually prints *truely*, which is not at all like it.

For *present* in l. 6, Tytler prints *pent*, which makes no sense, and loses a syllable. The transcriber did not understand the mark of abbreviation, as E. Thomson rightly observes.

I wil the schewe the more, I will shew thee the more.

107. This is a very difficult stanza. Tytler gives a loose paraphrase, hardly agreeing with his text ; and, in order to get a sort of sense, inserts the word *God* between *writh* and *alone*, without any hint that the word *God* is not in the MS., and without observing that the insertion upsets the scansion. The fifth line is evidently the one that is corrupt; and when we compare it with the second line in st. 120, the source of the corruption becomes clearer. In the latter case, I have little doubt that the right reading is *aughten*, written *aughtē;* that the Midland suffix *-en* was not understood by the scribe, and that he consequently substituted the abbreviation *&* for it. So here, I take *bynd &*, in the MS., to stand for *byndē*, or rather *bunden*, properly the past participle. I think it also tolerably certain that *mynes* is miswritten for *menys* (see st. 192), which would be better spelt *menes*, as in st. 111. By comparing all these stanzas together, this will appear more clearly. I therefore propose to read *with otheris bunden, menes to discerne*. I should then paraphrase the stanza thus: 'This is to say, though it pertain to me, in the law of love, to govern (or wield) the sceptre, so that the effects of my bright beams have their aspects by eternal ordinance, bound up (in their influence) with others [*i.e.*, with the aspects of other planets] so as to discern the means [viz., of obtaining results] at various times, both in things to come and (things) past — nevertheless it pertains not to me to direct events *alone*.' Briefly, 'I have certain powers, but they are bound up with the powers of other planets; I can discern ways of influence, at certain times; but I have no power to act *alone*, independently of the other planets.' In the next stanza, the same argument is continued. This is the best I can make of the passage ; perhaps some reader may be more fortunate.

Writh, to direct, control; lit. to turn and twist about. Cf. st. 122, l. 3, and see the Glossary.

108. The insertion of *by* improves both sense and metre. It means —'wherefore behold that, by the influence of other (planets), thy person stands not in liberty.'

Otheris must here mean other planets; doubtless Saturn would be included, as his effects were considered baleful. See Chaucer, C. T. 1330, 2458, &c. The influence of the moon would also be, in a measure, adverse ; see id. 2304, 2305 ; and also, perhaps, that of Mars, since Chaucer says (C. T. 2250) :—

> For, though so be that Mars is god of armes,
> Your vertue is so grete in heuen aboue,
> That, if you liste, I shal wel haue my loue.

Coursis, courses. This I take to be the right reading; for the long *s*, followed by a flourish, is sometimes used to denote *sis* as well as *se* or *ss*. There are several examples of this in the MSS. of Barbour. Tytler prints *course*, which leaves the line deficient.

Quhill of, &c.; till, by true service, thou hast won her grace. Tytler omits *graice*. The fact is that a line is drawn along above the word, as if to direct that it should be omitted ; but the scribe altered his mind, for he afterwards deleted this line by drawing three short strokes downwards across it ; it is, accordingly, to be retained. Still, it can be dispensed with ; in which case *hir I-wone* means 'won her.'

109. *Als like*, ye are as like, as day is to night; *i.e.*, not like at all.

110. The MS., in the second line, actually has *like vnto*, which Tytler prints without comment. Thomson well observes that *like vnto* is an error·for *vnlike to*, the *vn-* being in the wrong place. As to the unlikeness between January and May, it is much enlarged upon in Chaucer's Marchantes Tale.

Thaire tabartis, their coats are not both made of (one) pattern. If *tabartis* be allowed its three syllables, the word *maid* is not required. Tytler prints *tavartis;* the fact being that *b* and *v* are often made much alike in Scottish MSS. So again, in st. 116, l. 6, he prints *yvete* for *ybete*. In both cases we must read *b*, not *v*. The *tabard* was a short coat, without sleeves, usually worn by heralds, and displaying an armorial bearing. Hence the difference in appearance between the cuckoo and nightingale is expressed by saying that their coats-of-arms are not alike. This quaint idea is not at all stranger than Chaucer's assigning coats-of-arms to Theban knights.

To peire, to pair, pair off; *i.e.*, in goldsmith's work, a fish's eye is unfit to be paired off with pearl, or to be made of equal value with it (lit. to be made as high as it). For the word *peire*, I am responsible.

The word, in the MS., is written '*purerese*'; or it might be read as
'*pererese*' or even as '*prerese*'; all of which are nonsensical forms.
Tytler (against the MS.) prints *purcress*, of which he says: 'the word
itself, or its etymology, I don't find (*sic*) in any glossary.' We might
read *purchas with perll, i.e.*, to purchase a pearl with; but I prefer
peire, on the ground that only *one* syllable is needed; and I also think
that it makes better sense. I may add that, after deciding upon this
emendation, I found that Sibbald has the reading *pere* (be a peer to),
which is a doublet of *peire*.

111. *Othir mo*, others besides. Observe that *goddés* is accented on the
latter syllable; it stands for *goddesse* (observe the rime), and seems
to signify 'goddesses' in the plural. Venus is really alluding to
Minerva (see st. 112); and possibly to Fortune (st. 159).

To schorten with thy sore, to shorten thy grief with. This is the
usual position of *with*—viz., next to the verb. See notes to st. 16.
113. *Gude hope*, Good-hope, here an allegorical personage, and
Venus's messenger.

Joure alleris frend, the friend of you all. A better form would be
aller, as in Chaucer, C.T. 825, where *our aller cok* means 'cock for us
all,' lit. 'of us all.' *Aller* is for A.S. *ealra*, gen. pl. of *eal*, all.
Hence *alleris* is formed by the needless addition of the pl. suffix -*is*.
Tytler, not in the least understanding this, explains it by 'your ally,
associate, or confederate'; which later editors (except Thomson) have
carefully copied. Thomson says it is equivalent to Lat. *vester omnium
amicus*. But this is again wrong; for it is really equivalent to *vestrum
omnium amicus*. *Your* was originally the gen. pl. of the personal
pronoun.

To lette the to murn, to prevent thee from mourning.
115. *At thair large*, at large; as we should now say. In Chaucer,
C. T. 2290, Tyrwhitt prints, 'But it is good a man *to ben at large*';
whereas the right reading is *ben at his large*. It is easier to alter an
author's language than to understand it. Cf. notes to st. 181.

Is nocht eft none, there is not again (*i.e.*, even) one; an example of
the double negative. Tytler omits *eft none*, leaving the line two
syllables short.

Gevis charge, gives heed, pays attention.
116. *And for*, and because. The sense of this stanza is clear, but
it is difficult to fix the construction. The idea of it is borrowed from
the second stanza of Chaucer's Lenvoy a Scogan, especially the
lines :—

> But now so wepeth Venus in her spere,
> That with her teres she wol drenche vs here.

That ye se, which ye see beat so fast upon the ground. Tytler
prints *yvete*, which he explains by 'y-wet with my tears.' See notes
to st. 110.

117. *Stynten*, cease. This use of *stynten* in the *first* person of the present indicative is grammatically wrong; it is parallel to the misuse of *lakkith* in the same person, noticed in the notes to st. 27.

Men; here Tytler prints *me*, which upsets all the sense. After this word I have inserted *as*, to mend the metre. Such a use of *as* is quite idiomatic; cf. Chaucer, C. T. 87, 10859 :—

> And born him wel, *as* of so litel space.
> With so hy reuerence, *as* by his chere.

118. *Compacience*, sympathy.

119. Tytler puts a comma after *renewe*, and observes that 'the following verses in this and the next stanza are very obscure.' By removing the comma, we remove some of the difficulty. We may also supply a relative before *Most*. We then get some sense—viz., 'At that time folks always begin to renew that service unto love, which is ever due, (and which) most commonly has ever his (due) observance, and have repentance of their previous sloth.' If we might boldly substitute *That* for *Most*, it would be clearer.

Obseruance, i.e., homage, due reverence, is the right word here; cf. Chaucer, C. T. 1502 :—

> And for to don his obseruance to May.

120. The obscurity of this stanza is at once cleared up by changing *aught and* (in the second line) to *aughten;* the scribe would easily have misunderstood the Midland suffix *-en*, and seems actually to have made the same mistake elsewhere; see notes to st. 107. We then get *aughten maist weye—i.e.*, ought most to weigh, or pay regard. Thus the sense is : 'Thus mayest thou say, that my great influences, unto which ye ought to pay most heed, is all forgotten for sloth, (which is) no little offence; and therefore speak to them in this wise, as I have here bidden thee, and convey the matter which has been all the better expressed already.'

121. *Say on than*, continue then to say. Tytler makes here an excellent suggestion—viz., that Venus's complaint has reference to the wars of Henry V. in France, which, 'though glorious, had been disastrous both to France and England, and particularly to the nobility of both kingdoms.' Henry died on the 31st of August 1422; and the Kingis Quair was doubtless written in 1423, so that the reference to a period of mournfulness is very much to the point. Thomson (p. vi) cavils against this suggestion, because he thinks that James could have had no interest in the state of England. But observe the whole context, and remember that the lady Joan was English.

122. Cf. Chaucer, C. T. 2455 :—

> My dere doughter Venus, quod Saturne; &c.

Al hale, all whole, wholly, entirely.
Be tyme, betimes, in good time.
In l. 6, *with* helps out both sense and metre.

124. In l. 3, *hy* helps out the metre, and is a fitting epithet.

125. In Chaucer's Assembly of Foules, l. 242, we find that 'Dame Patience' is mentioned as sitting before the temple-door which the poet saw in his dream.

The said renewe; this, says Tytler, is unintelligible and must be wrong. By *renewe* we may understand 'renewal'; the chief difficulty is in *said.* Perhaps it should be *sad,* which is constantly used in the sense of sober, serious, sedate, grave, and is very fittingly applied to anything connected with Minerva. Perhaps we may take *sad renewe* to mean 'grave (*i.e.,* well-considered) renewal,' *i.e.,* sober fresh endeavour. But this is not very satisfactory.

127. *Prócure* must be accented on the former syllable. That it really was sometimes so accented, is clear from the poem of Alexander and Dindimus, ed. Skeat, where it is thrice spelt *procre.*

Fonde, to endeavour to obtain some comfort for thy penance at my hand. *Fonde* is not 'to find,' as Tytler says, but 'to try to find'; it answers to A.S. *fandian,* a derivative of *findan.*

128. *Anothir* is much better than *othir,* as in the MS.

129. *Of nyce lust,* upon foolish desire.

Gif the ne list, if it does not please thee.

130. *Him,* viz., God; as explained by the line following, 'who has the guidance of you all in His hand.'

132. *Bot gif,* unless.

And vtrid, &c.; we must certainly understand *bot gif* again before this clause. I suppose it to mean, 'and (unless) your word be uttered according to moderation (lit. by measure); (having regard to) the place, the hour, the manner, and the way, if mercy is to admit your service.' Tytler proposes to alter *vtrid* to *outrid,* which he explains by 'out-red, gone through, or regulated by measure and propriety, as to time and place.' But he does not tell us where he found *out-red,* nor why it means 'gone through.' There can be no doubt that *vtred* is the modern *uttered,* which sometimes meant 'published' or 'made known.' I had at first thought that we are to construe the sentence thus: 'and (unless) the place, hour, manner, and way be uttered (put forward) according to moderation'; for this is what the grammar would lead us to. I now suspect that L 6 stands alone, and is left, very awkwardly, without anything to govern the substantives. As to the 'circumstances' here referred to, see my notes to P. Plowman, p. 186.

133. Quoted from Ecclesiastes, iii. 1. Chaucer, C. T. 9846, says:—

For alle thing hath time, as sayn thise clerkes.

Abit, abides; short for *abideth.* So also, two lines below, *writ* is short for *writeth.* Such abbreviations are common in the third pers. sing. of the indicative; Chaucer has *abit,* C. T. 16643; *rit* (rideth), 976; &c. In the last two lines of the stanza, syllables must be supplied, as indicated; for the rime is a double one. The scribe probably thought the rime was single, and left out something accordingly.

134. *Hid*, hidden. Tytler simply omits this word, without a word of comment. It may be granted that it can be dispensed with.

135. *Lokin* is printed *lok in* by Tytler, as it stands in the MS. But it is certainly all one word, answering to A.S. *locen*, pp. of the strong verb *lúcan*, to lock. The simplest proof of this is that we have had the word already (with the prefix *i-*) in st. 69, where it rimes with *slokin* and *wrokin*. The sense is—'till she be fast locked amid his net.'

Fatoure, deceiver; Sibbald reads *feator*. Tytler actually prints *satoure*, which he explains by 'the lustful person'; Chalmers further explains that it means 'a satyr.' But there is no such word with the suffix *-oure*. Gower uses the word *faitour* more than once; Conf. Amant. i. 47, 65, &c.

136. Compare the description of the hypocritical falcon in the second part of Chaucer's Squieres Tale; and Gower's description of Hypocrisy in book i. of the Confessio Amantis.

137. *Ar suspect*, are suspected. Tytler prints *are*, but he makes no allusion to the MS. reading *and*.

139. *And wold bene he*, and should like to be the man.

Be him, by Him that died upon the cross.

140. The sense of this stanza is entirely lost by the mistake of the scribe in l. 5. For *Wald* we must certainly read *Nold*, *i.e.*, 'I would *not* be the man who should in any way be the blemisher of her good fame.' One wonders what the former editors supposed the meaning to be. The sentiment comes very near to that expressed in Chaucer's Book of the Duchess, 1262 :—

> That I *ne wilned* thing but good,
> And worship, and to kepe her name,
> Ouer al thing, and drede her shame.

141. Cf. Chaucer, C. T. 1489 :—

> This is theffect, and his entente plein.

Faynt, feigned, pretended. But this is not a happy expression; we should expect *faute*, *i.e.*, a fault. The last two lines mean : 'but so desire doth encompass my wits, (that) I regard no joy on earth except your favour.' For he means to say that Minerva's favour will procure him his heart's desire. Tytler puts commas after *desire* and *erth*, and has none after *compace*; but this gives no sense.

142. The fifth line, in the MS., is :—

> That day sall I neu*er* vp-ris*e*.

This is deficient and unmeaning; I therefore alter it to—

> That day sall neuer be I sall vp-ris*e*,

i.e., that day shall never come (when) I shall rise up (*or* make an attempt). Such a repetition of *sall* may have puzzled the scribe.

In balance, in jeopardy, in hazard, in risk. Cf. Chaucer, C. T. 16079:—

> I dare lay *in balaunce*
> Al that I haue in my possessioun ;

i.e., I dare risk all.

143. *For oure all thing*, for over, or above, all things (Tytler). Cf. Chaucer, C. T. 1120 :—

> The fresche beautee sleth me sodenly ; &c.

Hir worschip sauf, her honour being kept safe.

144. In l. 6, the insertion of *hir* improves both sense and metre.

145. In this stanza, unless the scribe has greatly erred, the words *duellyng, melling*, and *repellyng* are used to form but *single* rimes, the accent being on *-yng*. We may suspect that the scribe has ruined the metre.

Hir, her who has in hand the two lots, both of your weal and your woe. The allusion is to the goddess Fortune, introduced in st. 159.

146. In the second line, Tytler omits *all*, but curiously enough cites it in a footnote, so that the omission was an oversight. The only way to make sense is to read *Thar* for *Quhare* in l. 5. It then means : 'And how so be it, that some clerks declare, that all your lot is caused beforehand on high in the heaven, by whose great influences ye are more or less moved to (your) turning about—viz., there in the world (below), thus calling it [your lot] on that account (by the name of) Fortune, and so that the diversity of their influences should bring about necessity.' It is obscure enough, but the poet is handling a most obscure subject—viz., the question of predestination, and the contradiction between free-will and necessity. The whole is imitated from Boethius, bk. v. proses 2 and 3 ; whom Chaucer copies at great length in Troil. iv. 960, &c.; and playfully alludes to the same problem in his Nonne Prestes Tale (C. T. 15240), referring us to Boethius and Bishop Bradwardine for further information. The beginning of the next stanza resembles Gower, Prol. to Confessio Amantis (i. 22) :—

> That we fortune clepe so,
> *Out of the man himself* it groweth.

147. *In commune*, in common, in ordinary. Tytler, not understanding, as it would seem, the abbreviation for *com-*, oddly prints *qmune* (*sic*), both here and elsewhere.

Efter purpose, according to a purpose.

148. In l. 5, the substitution of *that* for *it* is obviously right.

Foreknawin is, is aware beforehand. It is the *past*, not the present participle. Cf. st. 45.

149. *Strangest*, strongest (not strangest).

150. *The schewit haue*, have shewn thee. *Haue* must be inserted.

151. 'Within a beam, which she, piercing through the firmament, extended from the divine country.' Tytler points out the accidental resemblance to Milton, P. L. iv. 555 :—

> Thither came Uriel, gliding though the even
> *On a sun-beam*, swift as a shooting star
> In autumn thwarts the night.

152. The passage included in stanzas 152-173 inclusive was edited by me, from the MS., with notes, at pp. 42-47 of my Specimens of English Literature from 1394 to 1579, first printed in 1871. Many of the notes are repeated here.

Maner soun, kind of sound. *Of* is always omitted after *maner* in Chaucer and other writers of the period.

153. *Can swym*, did swim, swam. This passage is imitated from Chaucer, Ass. of Foules, 183, &c. :—

> A garden saw I full of blosmed bewis
> Vpon a riuer, in a grene mede . . .
> With floures white, blewe, yelowe, and rede
> And colde welle stremes, nothing dede,
> That swommen fulle of smale fishes lighte
> With finnes rede, and scales siluer-brighte . . .
> And further, al about I gan espye
> The dredful ro, the buk, the hart, and hinde,
> Squirels, and bestes smale of gentle kinde.

Gesserant, not 'a precious stone,' as Tytler imagined, but a coat of bright mail. The scales of the fishes glittered like burnished armour.

154. '*An hye way*, I found there a way like as it were a high-way.' This again is like Chaucer, Ass. of Foules, 172, &c. :—

> For ouer al, wher I myn eyen caste,
> Were trees clad with leues, that ay shal laste,
> Ech in his kind, with colour fresh and grene.

155. *Fere lyonesse*, his companion, the lioness. *Fere* does not mean 'fierce or wild,' as Tytler says; that would have been spelt *fers*. The Earl of Surrey wrote a song to a lady that refused to dance with him, beginning "Eche beast can chose hys *fere*"; Tottel's Misc. 218.

Smaragdyne, emerald. Tytler wonders how the panther could be like an emerald. The fact is, that the poet follows the usual descriptions in the old so-called 'Bestiaries,' or descriptions of beasts. Compare, for example, the Bestiary printed by Dr Morris for the early English Text Society; the Bestiary of Philip de Thaun, in Anglo-French, printed in Mr Wright's Popular Treatises on Science; A. Neckam, De Naturis Rerum, ed. T. Wright; Solinus Polyhistor, and the like. In a description of the panther in the Codex Exoniensis, ed. Thorpe, it is described as being of various colours, *like Joseph's coat*. In A. Golding's translation of Solinus, b. i. c. 26, it is said of panthers that 'the hayre of their skins . . . is either white or *of a skye colour*'; and Neckam (p. 214) says the same. I suspect that our author is confusing the colour of the emerald with that of the sky. By way of further illustration, I here make a note that Chaucer, in his Assembly of Foules, calls the stork 'the wreaker of adultery'; the reason for which epithet is at once apparent on consulting Neckam's De Naturis Rerum (lib. i. c. 64), where the story is told at length.

The slawe ase, the slow ass, the drudging beast of pain, *i.e.*, of painful toil.

Werely, or *warlike* porcupine, armed with quills.—Tytler. It was said to loosen its quills, and dart them at dogs that pursued it; see A. Golding, tr. of Solinus, b. i. c. 42.

Percyng lynx; Neckam (p. 219) tells us that the lynx's piercing sight could see through nine walls !

Lufare vnicorn, lover unicorn. The descriptions in Neckam and Philip de Thaun show us why the unicorn (otherwise called *rhinoceros* or *monoceros*) is here called a *lover*. When the hunter wishes to catch a unicorn, he instructs a young girl to entice it; the unicorn goes to sleep with his head on the girl's lap, and then the hunter has him fast. Neckam gallantly remarks :—

> Rhinoceros capitur amplexu virginis : at quis
> Consimili renuat proditione capi ?

Voidis venym, dispels venom with his ivory horn. *Voidis* does not mean 'ejects,' as Tytler supposed, not knowing the story. The unicorn's horn was supposed to dispel poison ; Mrs Palliser, in her Historical Devices, p. 20, gives an example of a unicorn depicted as dipping his horn into water, with the motto *Venena pello*. In a footnote she shows that the *essai* of unicorn's horn is often mentioned in inventories. Cf. Massinger, Roman Actor, ii. 1. 46, and see E. Phipson's Animal Lore of Shakspeare's Time, p. 453.

156. 'There I saw the active tiger, full of cruelty, issue anew out of his haunt.' See *fery* in Jamieson ; Tytler misprints it *fere.*

Standar oliphant, the elephant that always stands. The elephant was said to have only one joint in his legs, so that he could not lie down. He used to lean against a tree to go to sleep ; see Philip de Thaun, p. 101 ; Golding's tr. of Solinus, bk. i. c. 32 ; E. Phipson (as above), p. 146.

The wedowis Inemye, the widow's enemy ; because he steals her chickens. See Chaucer's Nonne Prestes Tale, which is doubtless here alluded to, as is clear from the opening lines of it.

Clymbare gayte, goat that climbs.

Alblastrye, warlike weapons for shooting ; cf. *artillery*. Mr Chalmers suggests that the sinews of the elk may have been used for bowstrings ; I know of nothing to confirm this. In fact, I believe the true solution to be very different. The prep. *for* frequently means 'against,' or 'as a defence against'; see my note to P. Plowman, C. ix. 59. Hence *for alblastrye* means 'against warlike crossbow-bolts and darts.' Now 'shields and targets were made of the skin of the elk, which were thick enough *to resist the point of the sharpest spear';* E. Phipson, Animal Lore, p. 122.

Herknere bore, boar that listens, boar with keen hearing.

Holsum grey, badger, wholesome for hurts or wounds. Under the article *Grey,* in his Dictionary, Jamieson has the following note upon this passage: "I am informed, by a gentleman who has paid particular attention to this subject, that, in old books of surgery, badger's grease is mentioned as an ingredient in plaisters; undoubtedly as *holsum* for *hortis, i.e.,* hurts or wounds. He views the designation *herknere* as applicable to the wild boar, because he is noted for his quickness of hearing, and when hunted halts from time to time, and turns up his head on one side, to listen if he be pursued."

Haire, hare, that often repairs to the worts or vegetables. Tytler repeats *hortis,* instead of printing *wortis* here. Many plants were named after the hare, as *hare-bell, hare-mint, hare's-foot, hare's-lettuce, hare's-tail, hare's-ear,* &c.

157. *Bugill,* bugle-ox, who draws, &c. A. Golding's translation of Solinus, b. i. c. 31, tells us that bugles are "in manner lyke oxen, brystled, wyth rough manes on their neckes." See E. Phipson, Animal Lore, p. 134.

Martrik, marten. *Foynȝee,* beech-marten; F. *fouine.* The MS. is indistinct, and may be read *foynȝer,* but I think *foynȝee* is right.

Tippit, tipped like jet; viz., on its tail. *Noght say(is)* "*ho!*" never says *stop!—i.e.,* never ceases. The word *ho* is an exclamation, meaning 'stop!' see Chaucer, C. T. 2535.

Ravin bare, ravening or ravenous bear.

Chamelot; the camel, full of hair, (suitable for making) camlet. This statement is probably due to a popular etymology which connected *camlet* with *camel;* see the Glossary. At the same time, it would seem that camel's hair was really sometimes used in making camlet.

158. *To purpose,* to my purpose, to my story.

Furth, forth, along. To complete the line, it seems as if the *r* must be strongly trilled, so as to make *fur-r-th* dissyllabic; just as *pearl* is so in Burns.

In hye, in haste; a *very* common phrase in Barbour.

159. *Round;* perhaps *rounde,* dissyllabic.

Aspide must be read for *spide,* to complete the line; it is, in fact, the commoner form; see Chaucer, C. T. 13521.

Cleuering, clinging, clambering; holding on as a cat by its claws, which were called in Middle English *clivers.* As to the 'goddess Fortune,' see Boethius, bk. ii. pr. 1; Chaucer's Troil. i. 848, iii. 617, iv. 1, v. 1552; and Chaucer's Balade of the Visage [not Village] without Painting.

160. The fourth line is left imperfect. Instead of *and* (here denoted by the usual abbreviation, which occurs over and over again)

Tytler prints a *Q* turned upside down, adding, 'the reader's own ingenuity must supply this mark of abbreviation; perhaps it may be for *askew* or *askewis*.' This is too ingenious. All that we have to do is to *complete* the line, and I have no doubt that *of glewis* are the two omitted words. *Glewis*, lit. glees, also freaks, was the very word used with particular reference to the *freaks* or *tricks* of Fortune, or the *chances* of battle; see *Gle* in Jamieson's Dictionary.

161. The word *ermyn* seems to be trisyllabic; this may have been due to the trilling of the *r* (as *er-re-myn*).

Degoutit with the self, spotted with the same; alluding to the black tails with which white ermine is decorated. Cf. st. 157.

Chiere, demeanour, should have been spelt *chere,* as elsewhere.

It wold slake, it (her cheer) would leave off frowning.

And sche, if she; *for* must be inserted.

162. *Was,* which was; the relative being omitted. The MS. even omits *was.*

163. *Weltering,* rolling, turning. Fortune's wheel is represented as turning on a horizontal axis, whilst numbers of men cling on to it. As some clutch at it suddenly, or fall off into the pit beneath, it as suddenly turns round.

Strange thing, strange thing. Such is obviously the right reading, though the MS. has *strong.* This is because *strong* was sometimes written *strang;* see st. 149.

Clymben wold, wanted to climb; Tytler wrongly prints *clumben.*

164. 'And on the wheel [viz., near the highest point] there was a small vacant space, nearly stretched across (like an arch) from the lower to the higher part (of it); and they must be clever who long sat in their place there; so unsteadily, at times, she caused it to go on one side. There was nothing but climbing up, and immediately hurrying down; and there were some too who had fallen so sorely, that their courage for climbing up there again was gone.'

Fallyng is for *fallen,* the pp.; as in st. 45.

In l. 6, the omission of *so* before *sore* was due to the recurrence of the letters *s, o.* Cf. Chaucer, Troil. iv. 323 :—

> O ye louers, that hye vpon the whele
> Ben set of Fortune, in gode auenture !

165. *Hath (thaim) vp ythrungin,* has forcibly thrust them up again ; *thaim* must be supplied. In l. 6, we must supply *thought,* i.e., expected, hoped.

166. *Presence;* so in Tytler; MS. *presene.*

167. *Lyis the on hert,* lies upon thy heart.

Stant, stands, is. *Wald,* wouldest.

Endlang and ouerthwert, 'throughout my whole frame, in length and breadth.'—Tytler. The expression is taken from Chaucer's C. T. 1993.

168. *In poynt to mate*, on the point of being mated.   An allusion to chess, suggested by Chaucer's Book of the Duchess, ll. 620, &c.

> For fals Fortune hath pleyed a game
> *At chess* with me, alas ! the while . . .
> Therwith Fortunë seidë ' Chek here ! '
> And *mate* in mid point of the chekkere.

169. *Fundin stale;* Tytler prints *fund in* (though it is *fundin* in the MS.), and explains it by ' been long in ward, and sequestered from friends,' though he gives no reason for such a construction.   Still *fundin stale* means ' found a stall or a prison.'   I doubt if the expression *stale-mate* was in use at this period, else we might apply it to the poet's case, as he could not move from his place; but such an explanation seems to be barred by the use of the word *mate* above, which certainly means check-mate, not stale-mate.

Werdis wele, weal of the fates, *i.e.*, good fortune.

170. *Has stallit*, hast kept.

Be froward opposyt, by means of the perverse men opposite you. This refers to the idea of the wheel; the king is prevented from climbing up by enemies, of whom, however, Fortune prophesies that ' now shall they turn, and look upon the dirt,' *i.e.*, they will go past the highest point of the wheel, and fall forward into the pit below.   But this does not explain the hopelessly difficult phrase *quhare till aspert*, the meaning of which is unknown, and which must be corrupt.   Jamieson says *aspert* means ' rough,' from the Fr. *aspre;* but this does not help us one jot, nor does it account for the final *t*.   This *t* is the sign of a past participle, as if *aspert* meant ' exasperated,' from F. *asperer*, to exasperate (Cotgrave).   Hence *be froward*, &c., should mean ' by means of the perverse hostile men, whereunto (they were) exasperated.' Even this is very obscure, though less forced than any other explanation.

I may here observe that Jamieson quotes this passage s. v. *Dert*, and says that the sense obviously is ' dart a look on thee.'   But it is ' obviously' nothing of the kind; the king's foes, in falling head downwards, must have been wonderful men to succeed in darting looks on him during the process.

171. *Prime;* it runs past prime by an hour or more ; *i.e.*, the king's age was past *prime*, and the half of his life was ' near away,' as it is said in the next line.   He was already nearly thirty.   Fortune here compares his life to a day, which was nearly half done.   The hour of *prime* varied, but in Chaucer it sometimes means 9 A.M.; so here, an hour and more past 9 means nearly 11 A.M.   See the note on *prime* in my edition of Chaucer's Astrolabe.

172. *That fro*, those that from.

173. *Besy goste*, restless spirit.   This stanza is not imitated from the well-known dying address of the Emperor Hadrian to his soul, com-

mencing 'Animula vagula blandula,' as Tytler supposes; but is
directly copied from Chaucer's Troilus, iv. 302 :—

> O wery gost, that errest to and fro,
> Why nilt thou fleen out of the wofulleste
> Body, that euer might on grounde go?
> O soule, lurking in this woful *neste*,
> Fly forth out [of] my herte, and lete it breste . . .
> *Thy righte place is now no lenger here.*

Artow drest, art thou guided, or treated; lit. directed.

Walking, waking, whilst awake. So in Lyndsay's Monarché, b.
iv. l. 5551, we find : 'The Scripture biddis vs *walk* and pray.'

174. *Couert my-self*, 'within myself.'—Tytler. There is no authority
for this, nor is it quite the sense required. I suspect it is an error for
Towert, put for *towart*, or *toward;* which gives the right sense. We
find the spelling *towart* for *toward* in Barbour's Bruce, i. 83.

Sueuyng is, of course, an error for *sueuenyng;* the scribe lost his
place in the word. In l. 6, supply *I.*

My spirit with to glad, to gladden my spirit with. Cf. st. 190.

177. *Kalendis of confort*, 'beginning of comfort, a dawn of hope.'—
Tytler. See note to st. 34.

178. *List*, edge; Hooker has the expression '*list*, or marginal
border'; see Johnson's Dictionary. Tytler prints *lefe*, without any
hint that the MS. has *list* quite plainly; indeed, Sibbald so prints it.

I explain *branchis bryght and schene* with reference to the flourishes
with which the writing was ornamented; there was but *one* branch of
gilliflowers, on every edge (or available space) of which a sentence
was written in gold letters, ornamented with bright flourishes. It refers to the old style of illumination, so common in MSS. of the period.

179. *Bring the newis glad*, bring thee glad news. Observe that
news is plural.

Besid, close to, near to.

Present, presented; the past tense.

180. *Beddis hed*, bed's head. This was where Chaucer's Clerk kept
his books; C. T. 295.

181. *The quhich*, the which token truly, ever after, and day by day,
though it had at first mastered (*i.e.*, overwhelmed) all my wits, (yet)
from henceforth it did away the pains (of my grief). We must read
from hennesferth, as elsewhere, in st. 69, 144. Tytler prints *Quhich he
offerth;* the MS. has *Quhich hensferth.*

To quikin my lore, to quicken (*i.e.*, vivify, give life to) my learning.
Tytler oddly prints *qmkin*, the *m* being a little above the line (whence
Sibbald prints *quomkin !*); and, as this makes no sense, he puts a comma after the second *day*, another after *larges*, and informs us that *my
lore to my larges* is 'a proverbial phrase for I will exert my wit, to
make a return or recompence.' This is all invention; the sense is 'to
quicken my learning day by day, (so that) I am come again to my

freedom, (and) to bliss with her who is my sovereign.' This is an interesting allusion, as it tells us that at this time he obtained liberty to visit the lady Joan. With *to my larges*, compare *at thair large* st. 115.

Here the poem truly ends; the rest is an Epilogue.

182. *Apoun so litill evyn*, even upon so little; see st. 21. Tytler says 'upon so small an event.' Certainly *evyn*, as a spelling of *event*, is entirely unknown.

Croppin, crept. In the MS. the *r* is inserted above the line as a correction; Tytler, not knowing this, prints *coppin*, which he supposed to mean 'raised,' from M. E. *cop*, a top. This is impossible, because a verb formed from *cop* would be weak, and the pp. would be *copped*.

War croppin onys In hevin, i.e., had once crept into heaven, is extremely graphic; and the M. E. *crepen* (though now weak) was a strong verb, with pp. *cropen*, as in Chaucer, C. T. 4257. And, in another passage, where it is abbreviated to *crope*, it is used with *were;* see Chaucer, C. T. 11918.

Wald, &c.; would, after (uttering) *one* expression of thanks, utter six or seven more for joy. Tytler omits *o*.

I can say you no more; an expression caught from Chaucer; see, *e.g.*, C. T. 4595. Compare st. 187, l. 5.

183. *His goldin cheyne*, his golden chain. The chain of love, which binds together all things, is mentioned in Boethius, bk. ii. met. 8. Chaucer alludes to it in C. T. 2993; and in his Troilus, iii. 1744-1764.

Quhich thinkis; the MS. has *Quhich this*, which is nonsense; the scribe omitted a part of the word. The sense is, 'Let us see who, that expects to win his heart's mistress, would blame me for writing thereof' (*i.e.*, about Love).

184. This prayer for lovers is imitated from the Proem to bk. i. of Chaucer's Troilus.

185. *The dance of lufe;* Tytler misprints it *the dance of lyfe*, thus wholly missing the point; see note to st. 45.

186. *The rose;* a direct allusion to Le Roman de la Rose, where the courage required to pluck that flower is enlarged upon.

Spurn, trip against an obstacle, stumble.

187. *Lessen;* Tytler prints *lesseren*, but there is no such word.

It war to long, it would be too long. In l. 5, insert *you;* see st. 182, and the note.

The deth. By a singular coincidence, it was literally true that she defended the king when he was being assassinated. Tytler quotes the following: 'Having struck down the King, whom the Queen, by interposing her body, sought to save, being with difficulty pulled from him, she received two wounds, and he with twenty-eight was left dead.'—Hawthornden.

188. *Laud*, praise; Tytler prints *land*.

189. I supply *heye*, for the metre.

Glitteren; at first sight it looks like 'glat*eren*' in the MS., and Tytler so prints it; but wrongly.

190. *Hir with*, to gladden her with, ere that she went further (on her way). Cf. st. 174.

Mot I-thankit, may all other flowers be thanked !

191. *Sanctis marciall*, saints (of the month) of March. No other sense can be assigned here, and we must compare it with his former mention of the same month in st. 20; see note on p. 63. Hence we see that he thanks the saints of March, because that month was the 'first cause' of his good fortune, though it had formerly been the time of the beginning of his sorrows. But for his captivity, he would not have seen his love.

First fortunyt, it first happened to me, that my heart's remedy and comfort should appear.

192. The necessity for the insertion of *ȝit* in l. 7 is proved by comparison with l. 7 of st. 193.

194. The last four stanzas form the Envoy. Compare Chaucer, Troil. v. 1798.

Causing, causing (men) to know your simplicity and poverty. So also Chaucer, in his Troil. v. 1808, prays that no one may *mis-metre* him.

195. *In presence* is the right phrase, not *in the presence*, as in the MS., which spoils the line; it means, in general, to appear (as we should say) in good society. See Chaucer, C. T. 9083.

No wicht, no person, unless the mercy of her, who is thy guide and director, will admit thee (my poem) for the good-will she bears me; to whom do thou, on my behalf, piteously make entreaty.

196. The last three lines of this stanza, as they stand in the MS., are sheer nonsense. It is quite clear that a substantive must be supplied after *oure*, and the right substantive is clearly *lif*, or *fate*, or *weird*. Next, it is clear that *coutht* in l. 6 must be *couth*, for the passage is obviously imitated from Chaucer, C. T. 4614 :—

> For in the sterres, clerer than is glas,
> Is writen, god wot ! *who so coude it rede*,
> The deth of euery man, withouten drede.

Lastly, in l. 5, as the poet cannot *think* God (as in the MS.), it must be that he would *thank* God. With these necessary alterations, we get the following sense : 'Whom we thank, Who has written all our life, whoever could read it, many a year since, high in the circular figure of the heavens.' The reader must not omit to notice that the poet winds up this stanza by repeating the *first* line of the poem ; I have therefore marked it as if it were a quotation. The reference is to the old belief, that a man's horoscope was written in the heavens at his birth ; this is why he says, 'agone syne mony a ȝere.' See Chaucer, C. T. 4610.

197. *Impnis;* so in Tytler, though the MS. has *Inpnis*, which he does not tell us; however, it occurs again in st. 33, l. 3. The poet

says, ' I commend my book, (written) in (stanzas of) seven lines, to
(the protection) of the hymns of my dear masters Gower and Chaucer,
&c.; and, moreover, I commend their souls to the bliss of heaven.'
This commendation of his poem to the *poems* of Chaucer and Gower
is somewhat singular; it must mean that he wishes it to be understood
that he has been guided in his composition by their authority. In
how many places he has copied Chaucer more or less closely, has been
shewn in these notes; but I do not think it will be found that he owed
much to Gower directly. Still, we may take it to mean that he had
read and admired the Confessio Amantis, the reputation of which
stood much higher then than it does now. The indirect influence of
Gower appears nevertheless in the whole tone of his poem, which has
much of Gower's gravity and moralising, and very little of Chaucer's
lightness of heart and humour.

I may here mention that, in Prof. Morley's English Writers, vol. i.
pt. 2. p. 453, an additional stanza is given by some mistake. This
stanza is not in the MS. nor in the editions, and obviously belongs to
some other poem, since it speaks of Lydgate as being dead, though he
did not die till about 1460.

NOTES TO THE BALLAD OF GOOD COUNSEL.

THERE is no title to the original, but I call it " Good Counsel " because it is an obvious imitation of the " Ballad of Good Counsel " by
Chaucer, which begins, " Fle fro the presse, and dwel with soth-
fastnesse," and has for its refrain, " And truth thee schal deliuer, it is
no drede." Both ballads alike consist of three seven-line stanzas, the
last line in each stanza recurring without alteration. I print at length
three of the copies, with a collation of the fourth. They occur in the
following MSS. and books :—

1. MS. Kk. 1. 5, in the Cambridge University Library; already
   printed by Dr Lumby in his edition of Ratis Raving[1] published
   for the Early English Text Society.
2. The Bannatyne MS. in the Advocates' Library, Edinburgh.
   I am indebted to Mr John Small, of the University Library, Edinburgh, for a copy of this, collated with the MS. He informs
   me that it has been printed by the Hunterian Club (Glasgow.)

---

[1] This title is not explained by the editor; it means ' Rate's Raving,' *Ratis* being
the genitive case of the author's name, who pleasantly calls his poem 'a raving.'
MS. Ashmole 61 (Oxford) contains a collection of romances by a person of this
name.

3. The Gude and Godlie Ballates, 1578, reprinted by David Laing, in 1868 (p. 202). See a copy of it in Dr Lumby's notes to Ratis Raving, p. 119.

4. Ane compentiovs Booke of godlie and spiritvall Songs; Edinb. 1621, 8vo. See a copy of it in D. Irving's History of Scotish Poetry, 1861, p. 152.

From a collation of these copies, I have attempted to restore the text, though the variations in some places are too great to allow of certainty as to the right reading.

The following notes refer to particular words and phrases:—

2. *Noblay* is the right word, signifying nobility or noble rank. It occurs in Barbour's Bruce, 8. 211, 15. 271, and is contracted from O. F. *noblete*. In the later versions the scribes have spoilt the line in attempting to alter the word. The reading *nobill-ray* in version 2 may have arisen from the form *nobillay*, another spelling of *noblay;* see The Bruce, 9. 95, 17. 225.

3. 'Of any weal or of whatever rank thou be.' This seems to be the best reading, and merely requires the change of *of* to *or* in version 1.

4. *His steppis sew*, follow its steps. Here *his* is the genitive of the neuter pronoun, and refers to *virtue*. The old word *sew* has been translated in later copies by *persew* and *follow*, to the ruin of the scansion.

Dreid thee non effray, dread for thyself no terror. *Thee* is the dat. case. *Effray*, dread, fear, terror, occurs in The Bruce, 11. 250, 13. 270, &c., and answers to F. *effroi*. *Affray* is not quite so good a spelling, but is common, occurring in The Bruce, 3. 26, 6. 423, &c.

5. *Exil*, exile, banish; the reading *eject vice* gives a sad jolt to the rhythm. Such spellings as *wyce* for *vyce* are common in Lowland Scotch MSS.

6. *Thy luf began*, began by loving thee. Here *thy luf* means 'love of thee.' This use of *thy* occurs occasionally.

7. 'And for every inch he will requite thee (by giving thee) a span.' Alluding to the proverb—'Give him an inch, and he'll take an ell.' In Hazlitt's Proverbs, p. 142, this proverb is cited; and with it a quotation from Armin's Nest of Ninnies, 1608: 'Give me an inch to-day, I'll give thee an ell to-morrow.'

10. *Thy tym to compt*, thy time (when thou comest) to count it; *i.e.*, the length of thy life, when considered.

11. *Soyn;* I adopt this spelling of 'soon' from The Bruce (4. 126, 179, &c.) in preference to *sone*, in order to avoid writing a final *e*. It should always be remembered that final *e* seldom constitutes a syllable in the Northern dialect, and is best avoided in writing. We might write *soun;* we find *soune* in The Bruce, 1. 566. The line means: 'for green grass soon comes withered hay'; suggested by various passages in the Bible, such as James, i.

10, Ps. xc. 6; &c. Jamieson illustrates *walowit* from Douglas's Virgil (see Small's edition, ii. 127. 14, iii. 76. 10, 110. 11); Pinkerton's Select Ballads, i. 13; Wyntoun, i. Prol. 123; &c. The most interesting examples are to be found in Wyclif's translation of Mark, iv. 6, and James, i. 11: 'And whanne the sunne roos vp, it *welewide* for heete, and it driede vp, for it hadde no roote.' 'The sunne roos vp with heete, and driede the gras . . .; and so a riche man *welewith* in his weies.' It is the A.S. *wealwian*, to dry up, allied to G. *welken*, to wither, prov. E. *wilt*, to wither; and has nothing whatever to do (as Jamieson imagined) with the G. *falb*, E. *fallow*, or the Lat. *flauus*. The radical sense is rather 'to be rolled or shrivelled up'; cf. A.S. *wealcan*, to roll (whence mod. E. *walk*).

12. *Quhill licht is of the day*, whilst the light of the day remains, whilst daylight lasts. This is nothing but a version of John, ix. 4, and is the best reading. Indeed, the reading *quhilk suith is of thy fay*, *i.e.*, which is the truth of thy faith, gives no good sense. *Suith* is for *suth*, sooth; both sb. and adj.

15. *Sen word is thrall*, since speech is a slave; the author contrasts speech with thought, and calls it a 'thrall' by comparison with the freedom of thought.

16. *Thou dant*, do thou make tame; E. *daunt*, derived (through the French) from Lat. *domitare*. *That power hes and may*, that has power and is of might. Here *may* has the force of *can*, *i.e.*, has might. He alludes to James, iii. 8. Some editors wrongly put a comma after *hes*, and read this line in conjunction with the next, as if he meant 'and may thou shut thine eyes.' This is quite contrary to the usual habits of our old authors.

19. *Graip or thou slyd*, grope ere thou slip; *i.e.*, feel your way before you begin to slide into a ditch. This well suits the rest of the line—viz., 'and creep forth (go slowly forwards) on thy way; of which *and keip furth the hie way* is a corruption due to mistaking *creep* for *keep*, and so losing the sense. It will be noticed that version 1 has the curious word *stramp*, a strengthened form of *tramp*, to trample, tread, used by Lyndsay (see Jamieson). Yet it does not seem to be right, as it does not suit the context.

20. Here we are offered a choice of readings—viz.,

(1) Keip thi behest one-to thi lord, and thane :
(2) And keip thy faith thow aw to God and man :
(3) Thow hald the fast upon thy God and man.

The concluding words (*and thane*) of version 1 can hardly be right, because they require an *alteration* in the refrain or last line, which must begin with *and*, as before. Yet *behest* is probably right, being the old word for 'promise'; *faith* seems to be a translation of it, and *the fast* a substitution for it. And we must read *God* rather than *lord*, to agree with the preceding stanzas. Hence I would read: 'Keip thy behest unto thy God and man.'

GLOSSARIAL INDEX.

In the following Index, besides the abbreviations *s.* or *sb.*, *a.*, *adv.*, for *substantive*, *adjective*, *adverb*, &c., the following are used in a special sense: *v.*, a verb in the infinitive mood; *pr. s.*, present tense, 3d person singular; *pr. pl.*, the same, 3d person plural; *pt. s.*, past tense, 3d person singular; *pt. pl.*, 3d person plural. Other persons are denoted by 1 *p.* and 2 *p.* Also *imp.* is used for the imperative mood, and *pp.* for the past participle. The numbers refer to the stanzas. The references to "J." are to the last edition of Jamieson's Dictionary, 1844 (see further Remarks at the end of this Index, p. 113). The references to Barbour or The Bruce are to my edition of Barbour's Bruce, published for the Early English Text Society in 1870.

A, *prep.* on, in, 20.

A, one, a single, united, 64; A soyte, one livery, 64.

Abaisit, *pp.* abased, humbled, 41; Abaist, 166. F. *abbaisser*, "to debase, abase, abate, humble, depress, deject;" Cotgrave. J.

Abandoun, *adv.* left to myself, 25. Lit. at my free will. "*A bandon*, at large;" Cotgrave. J.

Abate, *s.* discomfiture, surprise, overthrow, 40. From F. *abatre*, "to fell, overthrow, defeat;" Cotgrave. J.

Abit, *pr. s.* abides, awaits, 133. So in Chaucer, C. T. 16643. See below.

Abyde, *imp. s.* abide, wait, 106.

Accident, *s.* incident, 191.

Accord, *v.* agree, 92; *pr. s. subj.* 132.

Adoun, *adv.* down, 53, 88.

Aduert, *v.* turn towards (me), vouchsafe, 25.

Aduertence, control, 108. Lit. power to advert to.

Affray, *s.* fray, struggle, 185.

Affrayde, afraid, 74.

After, according as, 79. See Eftere.

Agane, *adv.* again, 162.

Agane, *prep.* against, 29; Ageyne, opposing, 75.

Agit, aged, 83.

Agone syne, *adv.* long ago, 196.

Airly, *adv.* early, 23, 29.

Alawe, *adv.* down, below, downwards, 35, 154.

Alblastrye, *s.* crossbows and similar weapons; *For a.*, against shot, 156. A collective sb. from *alblast*, which is from Lat. *arcubalista*; see *Awblaster* in J. See note, p. 87.

Aleyes, *pl.* avenues, 32.

Alight, *pt. pl.* alighted, 61.

All day, *adv.* continually, 87. See note, p. 77.

Allace, *interj.* alas! 43.

Alleris, *gen. pl.* of all, 113. The suffix *-is* is superadded, as in *their-is*, theirs, *your-is*, yours, *our-is*, ours. *Aller* is the A.S. gen. pl. *ealra*, of all.

Allone, alone, 2.

Alluterly, *for* All uterly, all utterly wholly, 129. J.

G

Als, as, 109, 112.

Amaille, *s.* enamel; *fyre amaille*, fire-enamel, enamel produced by fire, 48. "*Esmail*, ammell or enammel;" Cotgrave. J.

Amaisit, *pp.* amazed, in a maze, perplexed, 73.

Amang, *prep.* amongst, 61.

Amang, *adv.* occasionally, at times, 66, 81; Among, 33. So in Barbour.

Amongis, *prep.* amongst, 91.

Amorettis, *pl.* (perhaps) penny-cress, 47. It means something to which a spangle can be likened, and therefore hardly 'love-knots, garlands,' as in J. See note, p. 69.

And, *conj.* if, 161. So in Barbour.

Anewis, *pl.* little rings, 160. Perhaps small twists; it seems as if possibly small buds or knops are intended. O. E. *anel, aniau*, a ring; Roquefort. Lat. *anellus.* J.

Anker, anchor, 100.

Anon, *adv.* anon, immediately, 166.

Ape, ape, 155.

Aport, *s.* demeanour, deportment, 50, 177. J.

Appesare, appeaser, pacifier, 99.

Aquarie, Aquarius (sign of the zodiac), 1.

Ar, are, 137.

Araisit, *pp.* raised, 75.

Arest, *s.* stop, 61.

Argewe, *v.* argue (with), 27.

Ariete, Aries, the Ram, 20. See the note, p. 63.

Armony, harmony, 152.

Array, *s.* garb, 110. *Maid of array* means "made of one pattern or garb." Perhaps the right reading was *a ray*, one array.

Artow, 2 *pr. s.* art thou, 58, 173.

As, that, 77; Quhare as, where that, 40.

Ase, ass, 154.

Aspectis, *pl.* aspects, 99.

Aspert, 170. Meaning unknown. Jamieson's suggestion, "harsh, cruel," from O. F. *aspre*, is impossible; for the word has a final *t* which cannot be thus accounted for. It might, however, mean "exasperated," formed as a pp. from a verb *asperen* = O. F. *asperer* (Cotgrave), to exasperate. See the note. Godefroy gives *aspert* as an occasional spelling of *apert*, open, noble, bold, also impudent. One difficulty resides in the awkward word *quhartill*, whereunto.

Aspide, *pp.* spied, 159.

Assay, *s.* trial, attempt, 89; Assayes, *pl.* proofs, trials, 137.

Assure, *v.* assure (myself), be sure, 140.

Astert, *v.* escape, 44; *pt.s.* started, 40.

Astonate, *pp.* astonied, 98; Astonait, 162.

At large, *adv.* at liberty, free, 38.

Atonis, at once, 68.

Atoure, *put for* At our, at over, above, 81. J.

Atyre, *s.* attire, 1, 46.

Auance, *v.* prosper, advance, help, help forward, 50, 79, 156.

Auenture, adventure, 22, 79; fortune, 10, 26, 95, 106.

Aught, ought, 120. Read *aughten* for *aught and*; see the note, p. 82.

Auise, *s.* advice, 114; Avise, 22, 150.

Avise, *v.* tell; On avise, tell of, 97.

Awayte, *s.* waiting upon (another), service, 121.

A-werk, at work, 4. Here *a* is for *on*.

Awin, *a.* own, 12, 108.

Aworth, *for* On worth, in worth, worthily, 6. So Tytler, who is quite right. Cf. the numerous examples of *a* for "on," *i.e.*, in, in Stratmann, s.v. *an*.

Axis, accession of sickness, attack of sickness, pain, qualm, 67. A bad spelling of *acces*, i.e., *access, accession*, sudden fit of illness. See *axes* in the Catholicon Anglicum. It is merely the O. F. *acces*; the etymologies in J. are both of them wrong. "*Acces de fiebure*, a fit of an ague;" Cotgrave.

Ay, *adv.* ever, 11.

Bade, 1 *pt. s.* remained, 72.

Balance, *s.* hazard, 142.

Balas, *pl.* balas rubies, 46. Cotgrave gives "*ballay*, a balleys ruby." Named from *Badakhshan*, which lies N. of the river Oxus.

Band, *s.* bond, bondage, 43.

Bare, *s.* bear, 157. (Better spelt *bere*; and *bore*, a boar (156) should rather have been *bare*; see *Bar* in Barbour).

Batailis, *pl.* battles, 85.

Be, *prep.* by, 20, 127, 139; owing to, 170; Be this day, as at this day, now, 69.

Be, *pp.* been, 175.

Becummyn, *pp.* become, 121.

Bedis, *pl.* prayers, 62. J.

Begilit, *pp.* beguiled, 90.

Begone, *pp.* circumstanced ; Wo begone, beset with woe, 30, 103 ; Wele is vs begone, things have happened well for us, we are well circumstanced, 64. For *wel begone*, see Chaucer, C. T. 6187. It is the pp. of *bego*. See examples in Mätzner's Old English Dictionary, p. 235.

Begonne, *pp.* begun, 34.

Begouth, 1 *pt. s.* began, 13, 16, 98. J. A false form ; see *Begouth* in my Glossary to the Bruce.

Behalding, *pres. pt.* beholding, 159.

Behest, *s.* promise, p. 54, l. 20.

Bell, bell, 11 ; Bellis, *pl.* bells (on the dog's collar), 53.

Beme, *s.* beam, 151.

Bene, 2 *pr. pl.* be, 109 ; *pr. pl.* 111. Put for *ar*, are, which is the *Northern* word.

Benevolence, good will, encouragement, 108.

Bere, *v.* bear, support, 131.

Beschadit, *pt. pl.* shaded, 32.

Besid, *adv.* close to, arrived at, 179.

Best, *a. as sb.* best course, 5.

Bestly, *a.* bestial, 136.

Besynesse, *s.* activity, 155.

Bet, *adv.* better, 101.

Beting, *s.* beating, correction, 122.

Beuer, *s.* beaver, 157.

Beugh, bough, 35 ; *pl.* Bewis, 32, 191.

Bill, *s.* bill, beak, 178.

Billis, *pl.* bills, petitions, 82. So in Piers Plowman.

Birn, 1 *pr. s.* burn, 168 ; *pres. pt.* Birning, 48.

Blake, *a.* black, 161.

Blamischere, blemisher, 140.

Blewe, *a.* blue, 153.

Blisfull, blisful, 100.

Blisse, *s.* bliss, 181.

Boece, Boethius, 3.

Bore, *s.* boar, 156.

Bore, *pp.* borne, 181.

Borowe, protection ; *to borowe*, as your protection, 23. See the note, p. 64.

Bot, unless, 69 ; Bot gif, unless, 132.

Bot, *prep.* except, 94.

Bote, boat, 18.

Brede, breadth, 21. See *Breid* in Barbour.

Bref, brief, 127.

Brethir, *pl.* brethren, 184. So in Barbour.

Brid, bird, 135.

Bridis, *pl.* brides, 65. See note, p. 73.

Brukill, *a.* brittle, 134. Der. from A.S. *broc-en*, pp. of *brecan*, to break.

Brukilnesse, *s.* frailty, 194. J.

Bugill, *s.* ox, 157. See *Bugle* (1) in my Etym. Dict. ; and note, p. 88.

Buket, bucket, 70.

Busk, bush, 135. So in Barbour.

But, *prep.* without, 8.

Bute, remedy, 69. A.S. *bót.*

Butles, without remedy, 70.

By, *prep.* with reference to, 16, 70.

Bydis, *pr. s.* abides, 65.

Bynd ; here *bynd and* (107) is an error for *bunden*, bounden, bound. See the note, p. 79.

Cace, *s.* lot, case, 143.

Cald[e], *adj. pl.* cold, 69.

Calyope, Calliope, 17.

Camel, *s.* camel, 157.

Can, *pr. s.* knows how to give, 106.

Can, *for* Gan, began ; *can him to comfort* = did comfort himself, 4.

Capis, *pl.* capes, 81, 88.

Capricorne, Capricornus, 1.

Caris, *pl.* anxieties, woes, 98.

Carolis, *pl.* carols, 121.

Cas, case, quiver, 94.

Cast, 1 *pr. s.* throw a stone, 60.

Certeyne, *a. as sb.* certainty, 138.

Cesse, *v.* cease, remain inactive, 59.

Chalk, *s.* chalk, 177.

Chamberere, chamberlain, 97.

Chamelot, *s.* camlet, a stuff, 157. Not connected, etymologically, with the word *camel.* Arab. *khamlat.*

Chancis, *pl.* adventures, 78.

Chapellet, chaplet, 97, 160 ; Chaplet, 95.

Charge, *s.* charge, 38 ; heed, 115.

Chere, cheer, good cheer, 81 ; cheerfulness, 36.

Chiere, *s.* countenance, 161. See above.

Chiere, *for* Chaire, chair, throne, 94. J.

Chose, *s.* choice, 92, 147.

Circulere, *a.* circular, 1, 196.

Citherea, *error for* Cinthia, the moon, 1.

Clap, 1 *pr. s.* clap, 60.

Cleo, Clio (muse), 19.

Clepe, 1 *pr. s.* call, 19 ; *pr. pl.* 149 ; Clepit, *pt. s.* 166 ; Cleping, *pres. pt.* 147 ; Clepit, *pp.* 3, 112. Used by Chaucer.

Cleuerith, *pr. s.* clambers, 9 ; Cleuering, *pres. pt.* clinging, 159. Better spelt *cliver* ; it is the frequentative of Icel. *klifa*, to climb.

Clippit, *pp.* embraced, surrounded, 75.

Cloistere, cloister, 90.

Clymbare, *a.* climbing, 156.
Clymben, *v.* climb, 163.
Come, 1 *pt. s.* came, 29, 158; *pt. s.* 154; *pt. pl.* 61. So *com* in Barbour.
Commune, common, 147; allied to, 149.
Commytt, *pp.* committed, 196.
Compace, *v.* encompass, 141.
Compacience, *s.* sympathy, 118, 150.
Compas, space, 96; circuit, 159.
Compilit, *pp.* compiled, 3.
Compiloure, compiler, 3.
Comprisit, *pt. s.* included, comprehended, 28.
Compt, *ger.* count, p. 54, l. 10.
Conclusioun, conclusion, determination, 13.
Condyt, *s.* conductor, 113.
Confort, *v.* comfort, 4.
Confort, *s.* comfort, 25, 123.
Connyng, *a.* skilful, 97; *s.* skill, 18, 50.
Conquest, *pp.* conquered, 100. See Barbour.
Consecrat, *pp.* consecrated, 33.
Consequent, *s.* result, 189.
Conserue, 2 *pr. s. subj.* keep, 112.
Constreyne, *v.* constrain, 116.
Contenance, *s.* demeanour, 45, 50, 82.
Contraire, *a.* contrary, 144.
Conueye, *imp. s.* convey, express, 120; Conueide, *pp.* conveyed, 104.
Conuoye, *v.* guide, 71, 101; Conuoye, Conuoy, *imp. s.* guide, 18, 103; Conuoyit, *pp.* conducted, 189. So in Barbour.
Conyng, *s.* coney, 157. For *conin*, variant of O. F. *conil*, from Lat. accusative *cuniculum*.
Copill, couplet, 33.
Coplit, *pp.* coupled, 92, 93.
Corage, *s.* courage, 164; heart, 38.
Couchit, *pp.* arranged, adorned, trimmed, 46. Borrowed from Chaucer, C. T. 2163.
Couert, 174. *Almost certainly an error for* Towart *or* Toward, *prep.* as regards.
Counterfeten, *v.* counterfeit, imitate, 36; Counterfete, 135.
Coursis, *pl.* courses, 108.
Couth, 1 *pt. s.* knew, 16; *pt. s.* could, 196. See Barbour.
Cowardy, cowardice, 89. Chaucer has *cowardye*, C. T. 2732.
Craft, skill, contrivance, 2.
Cremesye, crimson cloth, 109. F. *cramoisi*; see *cramesye* in J. See *crimson* in my Etym. Dict.
Cristin, Christian, 142.

Crokettis, *pl.* small curls, curled knops, 47. Inserted by conjecture; see the note, p. 70.
Croppin, *pp.* crept; *were croppin*, had crept, 182. Chaucer has *cropen*, C. T. 4257; the verb *to creep*, was once strong. See note, p. 92.
Crow, crow, 110.
Crukit, *a.* crooked, 195.
Cukkow, cuckoo, 110.
Cum; To cum, to come, future, 107. Sometimes written *tocum*, though this is unoriginal and needless.
Cum, *pp.* come, 192; Cummyn, *pp.* 185.
Curage, Courage, 80.
Curall, *a.* coral, 153. J.
Cure, *s.* cure, help, 84, 95, 100, 101; care, 22, 38.
Cure, *v.* cure, heal, 167.
Cuttis, *pl.* lots, 145. See Chaucer.

Dance of love, 45. See note, p. 69.
Dant, *imp. s.* tame, restrain, p. 54, l. 16.
Darre, 1 *pr. s.* dare, 140.
Dayes; *now on dayes*, now-a-days, 137.
Dayesye, daisy, 109 (trisyllabic).
Decretit, *pp.* decreed, 179. See *decreit*, verb, in J.
Dedely, *a.* deadly, death-like, 26. J.
Dedeyne, *pr. s. subj.* deign, 168. So in Barbour.
Dee, 1 *pr. s.* die, 57. Barbour has *de*.
Defade, *v.* cause to fade, dispirit, 170. Rare; the pp. *defadide* occurs in the Allit. Morte Arthure, l. 3305.
Defaute, *s.* defect, 194; Defautis, *pl.* 194. So in Barbour.
Degoutit, *pp.* spotted, 161. From O. F. *degout*, a drop; Cotgrave.
Degree, rank, 23.
Degysit, *pp.* disguised, 81. It occurs in P. Plowman. J.
Deis, *pr. s.* dies, 52. See Dee.
Delitable, *a.* delectable, pleasant, 154.
Delyte, *s.* delight, 41; Delytis, *pl.* pleasures, 6.
Departing, *pres. pt.* separating, 92; Departit, *pp.* parted, 124.
Depaynted, *pp.* painted, depicted, 43; Depeyntit, 96. Chaucer has *depeint*, C. T. 12884. J.
Derrest, dearest, 44. So in Barbour.
Dert, dirt, 170. [J. is wrong as to this word.]
Desate, deceit, 135.
Despeired, *pp.* despairing, 30.

Determyt, *pp.* determined, 13. J. has the verb *determe.*

Deuil, devil ; *in the twenty deuil way,* in the way of twenty devils, by all possible means, 56. See note, p. 72.

Deuise, *v.* tell, 12, 73.

Deuotly, *adv.* devoutly, 62.

Dewe, *a.* due, 119.

Deye, *v.* die, 86. See Dee.

Digne, *a.* worthy, 39, 135.

Direct, *pp.* directed, 62.

Dirknesse, darkness, 71.

Discord, *v.* disagree, 92.

Discriue, *v.* describe, 16 ; Discryving, *pres. pt.* 4. J.

Dispite, spite, malice, 87.

Displesance, unhappiness, sorrow, 82. J.

Disport, sport, pleasure, delight, 134.

Disseuerance, separation, 93.

Ditee, ditty, 36, 62.

Do, *v.* cause, make, 44, 69 ; Dois, 2 *pr. s.* dost, 166 ; Dooth, *pr. s.* makes, 44 ; Dooth me think, makes me think, 12 ; Do, *imp. s.* make, 60, 102.

Doctryne, teaching, instruction, 151. *Thy d.,* instruction of thee.

Doken, *pl.* docks, burdocks, 109. Here *doken* = A.S. *doccan,* pl. of *docce,* a dock (plant). J.

Dote, *v.* be foolish, be fond, 47.

Doubilnesse, doubtfulness, 18.

Dout, *s.* fear, 64, 71. So in Barbour.

Doutfull, *a.* fearful, timorous, 17.

Draware, *s.* drawer, one who draws, 157.

Drede, *s.* dread, doubt ; *withoutin drede,* without doubt, 130. So in Chaucer and Barbour.

Dredefull, *a.* timorous, 126. So in Ch. C. T. 1481.

Dremes, *pl.* dreams, 174.

Dresse, *v.* direct, turn, 156 ; Dressit, *pt. s.* prepared, 175 ; *pt. pl.* ad-dressed, 153 ; Drest, *pp.* ill-treated, afflicted, 173. With the last pass-age compare the phrase 'to give one a *dressing.'*

Dromydare, *s.* dromedary, 156.

Druggare, *s.* drudge, drudger ; *as a.* drudging, 155. J.

Dure, door, 75.

Ecclesiaste, Ecclesiastes, 133.

Effectis, *pl.* effects, influences, 146.

Effray, *s.* terror, p. 54, l. 4.

Eft, *adv.* again, 10, 53.

Efter, *adv.* afterwards, 181.

Eftere, *prep.* after, 3, 64 ; in hope of, 104. *Eftir* in Barbour.

Eftsone, *adv.* very soon, 159.

Eke, *adv.* also, 173.

Elk, *s.* elk, 156.

Ellis, *adv.* otherwise, else, 59, 63 ; Elles, 39.

Embroudin, *pp.* embroidered, *i.e.,* decked, 152. A false form ; the verb is weak. Read *embroudit ;* cf. Chaucer, Prol. 89.

Emeraut, *s.* emerald, 46.

Enditing, *pres. pt.* enditing, 7.

Enditing, *s.* inditing, 18.

Endlang, *adv.* along, 167.

Endlang, *prep.* along, beside, 152 ; Endlong, along, 81. So in Barbour.

Enprise, enterprise, 20. J. says 'ex-ertion of power,' which is probably meant. See *Enpriss* in Barbour.

Ensample, example, reason, 148.

Ensured, *pp.* made sure, 9.

Entent, intent, intention, 13, 56, 190.

Entere, *a.* entire, 62.

Ere, *s.* ear, 172.

Ermyn, *s.* ermine, 157, 161.

Esperus, Hesperus, the evening-star, 72.

Est, east, 20.

Estate, high rank, 3, 50 ; royalty, 94.

Euerichone, every one, 64.

Euour, *a.* ivory, 155. J.

Evin, *adv.* even, just, 21.

Evinly, *adv.* exactly, 177.

Evyn, *adv.* even ; *apoun so litill evyn,* upon even so little, 182. See Evin.

Exile, 1 *pr. s.* banish, 117.

Exiltree, axle-tree, 189.

Extendit, *pt. s.* extended, 151.

Eyen, *pl.* eyes, 8 ; Een, p. 54, l. 17.

Facture, *s.* shape, 50 ; mien, 66. "*Facture,* the facture, workman-ship, framing of a thing;" Cot-grave. The same word as E. *feat-ure.* The old editions have *faiture,* but the MS. has *facture.*

Fader, father, 122.

Faille, *v.* fail (of), lose, 26.

Faille, *s.* doubt, 48.

Fair, *a. as sb.* fair fortune, 190 ; Faire, fair one, 66.

Fair-calling, Salutation, Fair-wel-come, 97. See the note, p. 78.

Fallyng, *pp.* fallen, 164.

Falowe, fellow, companion, 23.

Fand, 1 *pt. s.* found, 77, 79, 125, 154. A.S. *fand,* pp. of *findan.*

Fantasye, fancy, 11, 37.

Fantise, *s.* feigning, dissembling, 142. "*Faintise,* dissembling, hypocrisie;" Cotgrave.

Fatoure, deceiver, 135. O. F. *faiteor,* from Lat. *factorem,* a doer, maker, agent. Hence it took up the sense of pretender, impostor. Spelt *faytour* in P. Plowman.

Faucht, *pt. pl.* (who) fought, 85.

Fay, *s.* faith, 59. O. F. *fei,* F. *foi.*

Faynest, *adv.* most gladly, 195.

Faynt, *pp.* feigned, 141.

Fell, *a.* cruel, 56, 100.

Felonye, *s.* evil-doing, 102; cruelty, 156. J.

Fer, *adv.* far, 22; Ferre, 45.

Fere, *s.* companion, mate, 155. A.S. *geféra.*

Fer-forth, *adv.* far forward, 25.

Fery, *a.* active, 156. J. Not 'fiery,' as Tytler explains it. It is merely from Icel. *færr,* able, strong, used rather in the original sense of active, "full of go," formed from *för,* pt. t. of *fara,* to go.

Fest, fast; *to fest,* too fast, very fast, 61.

Fetheris, *pl.* feathers, 35.

Feynit, *pp.* feigned, 36.

Figuris, *pl.* figures, 28. See note, p. 65.

Flawe, 1 *pt. s.* flew, 61.

Flikering, *pres. pt.* fluttering, 173.

Floure - Ionettis, *pl.* flowers of the great St John's wort, 47. This appears from the description of the plumes; see note, p. 70. "*Jaulnette,* hardway, St Peter's wort, square S. Johns grasse, great S. Johns wort;" Cotgrave. From O. F. *jauine,* yellow.

Flourith, *pr. s.* flourishes, 133, 193; Flourit, *pp.* flourished, *i.e.,* flowery, ornate, 4.

Flude, flood, 20.

Fonde, *v.* endeavour to obtain, 127. A.S. *fandian.*

Fone, *pl.* foes, 71. A.S. *fán,* pl. of *fá,* foe.

For, *prep.* as a defence against, 156. For examples of this use, see P. Plowman, C. 9. 59. So in Chaucer's Sir Thopas, we find "*for* percinge of his herte."

For, *conj.* because, 116.

Forby, *adv.* by, past, 30, 31. J.

Forehede, forehead; Thy forehede, thy face, *i.e.,* thyself, 106.

Foreknawin, *pp.* foreknown; *f. is,* is aware beforehand, 148.

Foreknawing, *s.* foreknowledge, 149.

Forfaut, *pp.* forfeited, 141.

Forfet, misdeed, 92 ; mischance, 129.

Forget, *pp.* forgotten, 120. A.S. *forgeten,* pp. of *forgitan.*

Forgit, *pp.* wrought, fashioned, 47; forged, 94.

Foriugit, *pp.* condemned, 3. "*Forjuger,* to judge or condemn wrongfully;" Cotgrave.

Forlyin, *pp.* weary with lying in bed, 12. See note, p. 80.

Forpleynit, *pp.* exhausted with complaining, 73. J.

Forquhy, wherefore, 108 ; because, 41.

Forsake, *imp. s.* refuse, shrink from, 63; Forsuke, *pt. pl.* denied, 89.

Forthir, further, 99, 190.

Forthir-more, furthermore, 114.

For-tirit, *pp.* wearied, tired, 30.

Fortunyt, *pt. s.* it happened, 191 ; *pp.* gifted by fortune, 133.

For-wakit, *pp.* tired out with waking, 11. J.

For-walowit, *pp.* tired with tossing about, 11. See p. 61.

Forwepit, *pp.* exhausted with weeping, 73. J.

Foting, *s.* footing, 9.

Foynȝee, *s.* beech-marten, 157. "*Fouinne,* the foine, wood-martin, or beech-martin;" Cotgrave. J.

Fremyt, *a.* strange, unfortunate, unlucky, 24. J. A.S. *fremede,* estranged from.

Fret, *pt. pl.* adorned, 35. A.S. *frætwian,* to adorn.

Fret-wise, in fashion of adornment, 46.

Fricht, *pp.* frightened, 162.

Fro, *prep.* from, 52, 173.

Froward, *a.* froward (people), 170.

Fude, food, 30.

Fundin, *pp.* found, 169.

Furrit, *pp.* furred, 161.

Furth, *adv.* forth, away, 67 ; thenceforward, 13.

Furth, *prep.* forth, beyond, 158.

Furthward, *adv.* forward, 17.

Furth-with-all, furthermore, 13.

Fynnis, *pl.* fins, 153.

Game, *s.* amusement, *hence* happiness, pleasure, 17.

Gan, 1 *pt. s.* did, 10, 42 ; *pt. pl.* Gan to smert, did smart, 8.

Gardyng, *s.* garden, 33.

Gayte, *s.* goat, 156. Icel. *geit.*

Gerafloure, *s.* gillyflower, 190. *"Giro-flée,* a gilloflower; and most pro-perly, the clove gilloflower;" Cot-grave. See Iorofllis.

Gesserant, *s.* a coat or cuirass of fine mail, 153. *"Jaseran,* a coate or shirt of great and close-woven maile;" Cotgrave. See *Jazerans* in Roquefort, and *Gesserawnte* in Halliwell.

Geue, *v.* give, 172; Gevis, *pr. s.* gives, 115; Gevin, *pp.* given, 92.

Geve, *conj.* if, 195. Bad spelling of *gif.*

Gif, if, 28, 60; Giff, 141; *badly spelt* Geve, 195.

Gilt, *s.* guilt, 56, 137.

Gilt, *pp.* sinned, 26, 38. A.S. *gyltan.*

Girt, *pp.* girded, 49.

Glad, *v.* gladden, 174; Glade, 62.

Glad, *s.* gladness, 21.

Glewis, *pl.* destinies, 160. Supplied by me to fill up the line, which is left imperfect. *Glew* means 'for-tune of war' in Barbour, 6. 658. This is just what is meant.

Glitteren, *pr. pl.* glitter, 189.

Goddes, *pl.* gods (*perhaps* goddesses, *the accent being on the latter syl-lable*), 111; Goddis, gods, 123.

Gone, *v.* go, advance, 131; walk about, 103; *pp.* past, 107.

Goste, *s.* spirit, 173.

Gouernance, *s.* control, influence, 122; conduct, 88, 130.

Graip, *imp. s.* feel your way, p. 54, l. 19.

Gree, degree, rank, 83; victory, 59; Greis, *pl.* degrees, 21. J.

Gref, grief, 127.

Gres, *s.* grass, p. 54, l. 11.

Greuance, grief, 118.

Grey, *s.* gray, badger, 156. J.

Grippis, *pl.* grips, grasp, 171.

Ground, foundation, 6.

Ground, 2 *pr. s. subj.* found, 142; Groundit, *pp.* grounded, 138.

Gruch[en], *pr. pl.* complain, repine, 91. J.

Grundyn, *pp.* ground, sharpened, 94.

Gude, *s.* goods, 139.

Gude, *a.* good, 20.

Gudeliare, *adj. comp.* goodlier, 49.

Gudelihede, *s.* fairness, beauty, 49.

Guerdoun, *s.* guerdon, 193.

Gyde, *s.* guide, 113; Gyd, 195.

Gyde, *v.* guide, 15.

Gye, *v.* guide, 15, 106.

Gynneth, *pr. s.* begins, 17; Gynnis,

2 *pr. s.* beginnest, *hence* dost, 57; Gynnen, *pr. pl.* begin, do, 119.

Hable, *a.* able, fit, liable, 14; power-ful, 99. J.

Hable, *v.* enable, 39.

Hailith, *pr. s.* hales, draws, 70. J.

Hailsing, *pres. pt.* saluting; greeting, 166. See *Hailsed* in additions to J.

Haire, *s.* hare, 156.

Hald, 1 *pr. s.* hold, 60; Halden, *pr. pl.* maintain, 147; Haldin, *pp.* kept, 90.

Hale, *a. as adv.* wholly, 58, 74, 101, 122.

Hale, *v.* haul, pull, 169.

Halely, *adv.* wholly, 188.

Halfdel, *for* Half del, half part, half, partly, 89.

Halflyng, *adv.* partly, 49. J.

Hand; In his hand, held by the hand, 79.

Hang, *pt. s.* hung, 48; *pt. pl.* 81, 94. See Hingen.

Hap, *s.* good fortune, 133.

Hapnit, *pt. s.* happened, befell, 187.

Happily, *adv.* haply, perchance, 59.

Hardy, hardy, stout, 89.

Hare, *s.* hair, 157.

Has, *pl.* have, 107; Hastow, hast thou, 57.

Haunt, *s.* lair, 156.

Havin, haven, 100.

Hed, head, 160; Hedis, *pl.* heads, 79, 80.

Hedit, headed, 95.

Hele, *s.* health, healing, cure, 74, 169, 191.

Helle, *s.* hell, 162.

Henn[e]sfurth, henceforth, 69; Hen-[ne]sforth, 144; Hen[ne]sferth, 181.

Hent, 1 *pt. s.* seized, 180.

Herbere, garden for herbs and flowers, garden-plot or bed, 31, 32. Jamieson says, "it would seem that it is used for arbour by James I." Cer-tainly not; no arbour is ever planted with junipers. From Lat. *her-barium,* through the French.

Here, *imp. s.* hear, 148.

Herknere, *s. used as a.,* listening, 156. See note, p. 88.

Hert, *s.* heart, 40.

Hert, *s.* hart, 157.

Hertly, *a.* cordial, 121; *adv.* heartily, 144.

Hes, *pr. s.* has, p. 54, l. 16.

Hestis, *pl.* behests, commands, 112.

Heved, *pt. s.* heaved, uplifted, 1.

Hevynnis, *pl.* heavens, joys, 34.
Hewis, *s. pl.* colours, hues, 160.
Heye, high, valuable, 110; loud, loudly, 66.
Hicht, *s.* height, raising, 172.
Hider, *adv.* hither, 166.
Him, *dat.* on him, 6.
Hingen, *pr. pl.* hang, 88. See Hang.
Hippit, *pt. pl.* hopped, 35. J.
Ho, *interj.* ho! stop! 157. *I.e.*, he never stays 'stop' to murder. J.
Hole, *a.* whole, 18, 126; *s.* 171.
Holsum, *a.* wholesome, 156.
Hong, *pt. s.* hung, 160. See Hingen, Hang.
Hony, *a.* sweet as honey, 117.
Hore, hoary, 80, 83.
Hornis, *pl.* horns, 157; (of the moon), 1.
Hortis, *pl.* hurts, wounds, 156. See note, p. 88. J. gives *hort*, *v.* to hurt.
Hound, *s.* hound, dog, 53.
Hudis, *pl.* hoods, 81, 88.
Hufing, *pres. pt.* hovering about, dwelling, 159. See *hove* in J.
Huke, *s.* frock, dress, 49. "Huke, *surquanie, froc;*" Palsgrave. Cotgrave explains *surquenie* or *souquenie* by "frock, gaberdine." Skelton has it, in *Elynour Rummyng*, l. 56.
Humily, *adv.* humbly, 106, 176.
Humylnesse, humility, 126.
Hyare, higher, 131.
Hye, *a.* high; Hye way, highway, 154.
Hye, haste; *only in phr.* In hye, in haste (very common in The Bruce), 30, 75, 77, 158, 171, 177.
Hye, *v.* hasten, hie; 15, 164.
Hyndrit, *pp.* hindered, 137.
Hyng, *pr. pl.* hang, 89. See Hingen, Hang, Hong.

I-, *prefix; used in the pt. t.* Iblent, *and in the pp.* I-fallyng, I-laid, I-lokin, I-thankit, I-wone. This prefix is unknown to the Northern dialect, and due to imitation of Chaucer. Other examples are Ybete, &c.; see Y-, *prefix.*
Iangill, *v.* jangle, talk, 38.
Iblent, *pt. s.* became blinded, 74. See note, p. 74.
Ielousye, jealousy, 87.
Ienepere, *s.* juniper, 32.
Iete, *s.* jet, 157.
I-fallyng, *pp.* fallen, 45. *Put for* I-fallyn.
Ilaid, *pp.* laid, 120.
Ilk, *a.* same, 163; Ilke, 154.

Illusioun, illusion, 12.
Ilokin, *pp.* locked, enclosed, 69. See Lokin.
Impnis, *pl.* hymns, poems, 196. See Ympnis.
Incidence, incidental matter, 7.
Indegest, *pp.* undigested, crude, 14.
Inemye, *s.* enemy, 156; Inymyis, *pl.* 24.
Infelicitee, misfortune, 4.
Infortunate, *a.* unfortunate, 24.
Infortune, misfortune, 5, 45.
Inmytee, enmity, 87.
Iorofflis, *pl.* gilly-flowers, 178. See Gerafloure.
I-thankit, *pp.* thanked, 190.
Iuge, judge, 82.
Iunyt, *pp.* joined, 133. J.
I-wone, *pp.* won, 108.

Kalendis, *pl.* Kalends, beginnings, 34, 177. See note, p. 67.
Kepe, 1 *pr. s.* care for, regard, 141.
Kest, 1 *pt. s.* cast, 35, 40; *pt. s.* 104.
Keye, key, 100. But he means 'helm.' On this curious error, see the note.
Kid, *pp.* made known, manifested, 137. Spelt *kydd* in J. Used as *pp.* of *kythe.*
Knawe, *v.* know, 128.
Knawing, *s.* knowledge; *tofore knawing*, knowledge beforehand, foreknowledge, 148.
Knytt, *v.* strengthen, 194; Knet, *pp.* knit, twined, 31.
Kynd, *s.* kind, nature, 27, 35, 139.
Kythit, *pp.* manifested, shewn, 56. See Kid. A.S. *cythan*, to make known.

Lak, *s.* want, 15.
Lakkith, 1 *pr. s.* lack, 27. An error for *lakkis*, the Northumbrian form; see the note. Lakit, 1 *pt. s.* lacked, 16; Lakkit, *pt. s.* lacked, 84.
Lampis, *pl.* lamps, i.e., stars, 72.
Lang, long, 73; Langer, *adv.* longer, 10, 11, 68.
Langis, *pr. s.* belongs, 106, 107; Langith (Southern form), belongs (to), 114. J.
Lanternis, *pl.* lanterns, 19.
Lap, *pt. pl.* leapt, 153.
Largesse, *s.* bounty, 50; liberty, 183; Larges, liberty, 181. J.
Lat, 1 *pr. s.* let, 7, 187; *imp. s.* 99.
Latting, *s.* letting, 41.
Lauch, *imp. s.* laugh, 179.
Laud, *s.* praise, 188.

Laureate, *a.* laureate, 197.
Lawe, low, 90; below, 103.
Layes, *pl.* lays, 85.
Lede, *s.* lead, 153.
Lemyng, *pres. pt.* shining brightly, 46. From A.S. *léoma,* a ray of light. (Not allied to *gleam,* as J. wrongly supposes.)
Lent, 1 *pt. s.* leaned, 42, 73, 74, 191.
Lenth, length, 21.
Lere, *v.* learn, 171. (Misused; the M.E. *leren* means to teach.)
Lest, *s.* pleasure, desire, 57. J.
Lest, *pr. s. impers.* it pleases, 9; *pt. s. impers.* pleased it, 44; *pr. s. subj. impers.* may please, 147. J.
Leste, least, 149.
Lestnyt, 1 *pt. s.* listened, 11.
Lesty, *a.* skilful, 157. J. has *list,* agile. From A.S. *list,* art. See *liste* in Stratmann.
Lete, *pt. s.* let, 125. See Lat.
Let[te], *v.* hinder, stop, 113.
Leue, *s.* leave, 124.
Likit, *pt. s. impers.* it pleased, 7, 126.
List, *impers. pr. s.* it pleases, 78, 101; *pr. s.* is pleased, 25, 34; *pr. pl.* are pleased, 115; 2 *pr. s.* art pleased, 58.
List, *s.* edge, border, 178. "*Liste,* a list, or selvedge;" Cotgrave.
Long, *a.* long, 160.
Lokin, *pp.* locked, enclosed, 135. A.S. *locen, pp.* of the strong verb *lúcan.* See Ilokin.
Lore, instruction, knowledge, 111, 128, 149; learning, 181.
Louring, *adj.* louring, frowning, 161. See additions to J.
Louse, *a.* loose, 49, 115.
Louse, *v.* loosen, 39, 43.
Lowe, *s.* flame, fire, 48. Icel. *log.* J.
Lufar, *s.* lover, 179; Lufare (see note, p. 87), 155.
Lufis, *s. gen.* love's, 45.
Luke, *s.* glance, 51.
Luke[n], *v.* look, 170; Lukit, *pp.* looked, given heed, 25.
Lust, *s.* pleasure, delight, dear one, 65.
Lusty, *a.* pleasant, 121. J.
Lyf, person, 12. See Lyvis.
Lyght, *v.* alight, 177.
Lynx, 155. See note, p. 87.
Lyonesse, *s.* lioness, 155.
Lyoun, *s.* lion, 155.
Lyte, *a.* little, 13, 120; A lyte, a little, loosely, 49; *as sb.* little, 16, 161; little while, 2, 41. A.S. *lyt.* See *Lite* in J.

Lyue, life; On lyue, alive, lit. 'in life,' 84.
Lyvand, *pres. pt.* living, 197.
Lyvis, *s. gen.* being's, man's, 28. See Lyf.

Mach, match, 109.
Magnificence, *s.* greatness, 196.
Maidenhede, maidenhood, virginity, 55.
Maist, *adv.* most, 120, 182.
Maister, master, 125.
Maistrit, *pp.* mastered, overpowered, 181.
Maistry, *s.* dominion, mastery, 59; Maistrye, power, 37; By m., by force, 92; For m., as a masterpiece, 66.
Make, mate, companion, 58, 79; Makis, *pl.* 35, 64, 86. J.
Maked, *pp.* made, 110.
Man, lover, 63, 101, 187.
Menace, *s.* threat, menace, 41; Doith menace, offers menace to, threatens, 96.
Maner, *s.* kind, sort (of), 161.
Mantill, *s.* mantle, 160.
Marciall, *a.* Martial, *i.e.,* of the month of March, 191. See note, p. 93.
Martrik, *s.* marten, martin, 157. J.
Marye, *gen.* Mary's, 17.
Mate, *s.* checkmate, 169.
Mate, *v.* to be checkmated, 168.
Mater, matter, circumstance, 18.
Matyns, *pl.* matins, 11.
Maugre, *adv.* in spite of (us), 24.
May, *pr. s.* is able, is of might (to do harm), p. 54, l. 16.
Melling, *s.* interference, 145. J.
Mellit, *pp.* mingled, 152. J. From O. F. *mesler.*
Mene, *s.* mean, means, 183; Menes, *pl.* means, 111; Menys, 192.
Menen, *pr. pl.* mean, 137.
Merci, mercy, 34.
Merciable, merciful, 99.
Mesure, *s.* measure, moderation, 50, 51, 132.
Met, 1 *pt. s.* dreamt, 73. A.S. *mǽtan.*
Mete, *a.* meet, fit, 97.
Metir, metre, 4.
Mich, *a.* much, 51, 150.
Mineruis, *gen.* Minerva's, 124.
Minister, *v.* administer, perform, 43.
Mo, *adj. pl.* more (in number), besides, 42, 61, 97, 111, 157. A.S. *má.*
Moch, much; To m., too much, excess, 87.

Mone, moon, 110.

Mone, moan, plaint, 72. See Moon.

Monethis, *pl.* months, 65.

Monyfald, manifold, a great deal, 131.

Moon, *s.* moan, complaint, 45. See Mone.

Moralitee, *s.* morality, 4, 197.

Mornis, *pl.* mornings, 29.

Morowe, *s.* morning, 49 ; A morow, in the morning, 20.

Mot, *pr. s. subj.* may, 190 ; Mote, *imp.* 3 *p.* may (He), 71 ; Most, must, 15.

Moving, *pres. pt.* considering, 177.

Murn, *v.* mourn, 113 ; Murnyth, *pr. pl.* 118.

Murthir, *s.* murder, 157.

My, of me ; My disdeyne, disdain of me, 115. A.S. *min,* gen. of *ic,* I.

Mylioun, million, 78.

Mynd, remembrance, 2 ; memory, 85; Mynde, remembrance, 58, 151.

Mynes, *for* Menes, *pl.* means, 107.

Mynt, 1 *pr. s.* aim, 105. A.S. *myntan,* to determine, intend. See *mint* in J.

Na, not, 67.

Namly, *adv.* especially, 10.

Nap, *v.* take a nap, nod, sleep, 60.

Nas, *for* Ne was, was not, 75.

Nat, not, 10.

Nay, nay, i.e., otherwise, not so, 89.

Necessitee, necessity, 146.

Nest, *s.* nest, 173.

Newe, *adv.* newly, 8.

Newis, *pl.* news, 179.

Noblay, *s.* nobility, p. 54, l. 2. See note, p. 95.

Nothing, in no respect, 90.

Nouthir, neither, 139.

Nowmer, number, 19, 22, 81. J.

Nyce, *a.* foolish, 129 ; full of tricks, 155. See *Nice* in J.

Nycely, *a.* foolishly, 12.

Nye, nigh, 77.

Nyl, 1 *pr. s.* will not, 142.

O, one, a single, 182.

Observance, *s.* observance, due regard, 119.

Of, *prep.* of, by, 52 ; by means of, 108 ; from, out of, 93 ; upon, 129 ; with, 95 ; Off, by, 24 ; Off, from, 23.

Offense, offence, 38.

Oliphant, *s.* elephant, 156. J.

Omere, Homer, 85.

On, *prep.* on, with, 33. *Perhaps we should read* of.

One, alone ; By thame one, alone by themselves, 80.

Ones, *adv.* once, 57.

Ony, any, 8, 67. J.

Opnyt, *pt. pl.* opened, 21.

Opposit, (people) opposed (to you), 170.

Or, *adv.* ere, 180, 190 ; Or euer, ere ever, 5.

Ordour, *s.* order, 125.

Orfeuerye, *s.* goldsmith's work, 48. "*Orfevrerie,* the goldsmith's trade or work ;" Cotgrave.

Orisoun, orison, 53.

Ornate, *a.* flowery, 197.

Ouer, *prep.* besides, 61.

Ouercom. *pp.* overcome, 41.

Ouerthrawe, *pp.* overthrown, 163.

Ouerthwert, *adv.* across, 82, 167. Spelt *ourthort* in J.

Ouerwent, *pp.* pervaded, 74.

Oure, *prep.* over, above, 143. See Ouer.

Oure-hayle, *v.* overhaul, reconsider, 10 ; Oure-hailing, *pres. pt.* considering, 158.

Oure-straught, *pp.* stretched across, 164.

Ourset, *pp.* overset, upset, 73. J.

Out of, after, 4.

Pace, *s.* step, hence, a layer or stage in building, 131.

Pace, *v.* pass away, 69. See note ; and see Pas.

Pall, *v.* appal, amaze, make dull, 18. Short for *appal.*

Pantere, *s.* panther, 155.

Pape-Iay, popinjay, parrot, 110. J.

Part, *v.* depart, 67 ; Partit, *pp.* awaked, 2.

Partye, *s.* match, bride, 48 (see note, p. 71); In partye, partly, 16.

Pas, *v.* pass, go, 22. See Pace.

Paynis, *pl.* pains, 181.

Peire, *v.* pair ; To peire with, to pair off with, to compare to, 110. See note, p. 80.

Pennance, *s.* penance, 176.

Pepe, *interj.* peep ! cry of a bird, 57.

Percyng, *pres. pt.* piercing, 103 ; sharp-sighted, 155.

Perfyte, perfect, 125.

Perll, pearl, 110 ; Perllis, *pl.* 46.

Perseuerance, *s.* perseverance, 185.

Pertene, *pr. s. subj.* pertain, 107.

Pertynent, *a.* pertinent, pertaining, 138.

Phebus, the sun, 72.

Philomene, nightingale, 62 ; Phylo-
mene, 110.

Pitouse, piteous, 118.

Pitously, *adv.* piteously, 53, 73.

Plane, *s.* plain, 152.

Planet, planet, 99.

Playntis, *pl.* complaints, 82, 92.

Plesance, pleasure, 26 ; happiness, 93;
delightful appearance, 82 (cf. 90). J.

Plesandly, *adv.* pleasantly, 178. J.

Pleyne, *a.* plain, evident, 116.

Pleyne, *v.* play, disport, 40. Put for
Pleyen, Southern infinitive of *pley.*

Pleyne, *ger.* to complain, 90 ; 1 *pr. s.*
complain, 70.

Plumys, *pl.* plumes, 46.

Plumyt, *pp.* plumed, feathered, 94.

Plyte, *s.* plight, 53.

Poetly, *a.* poetlike, poetical, 4.

Polymye, Polyhymnia, 19.

Porpapyne, *s.* porcupine, 155.

Port, gate, 77 ; harbour, 17.

Portare, porter, 125.

Pouert, poverty, 3, 5.

Poure, *v.* pore, gaze, 72.

Poynt, *s.* point ; In poynt, on the
point of, 168.

Prattily, *adv.* prettily, 153.

Pray, prey, 135.

Prentissehed, apprenticeship, 185.

Presence, *s.* presence, 195. See
note, p. 93.

Present, *a.* present, 106.

Present, *pt. s.* presented, 179.

Prime, *s.* the prime hour of the day,
9 o'clock in the morning, 171.

Princes, princess, 99, 141.

Prise, *s.* praise, 128, 188. See *priss*
in additions to J.

Processe, procedure, course of things,
126 ; course of time, 114, 143, 192 ;
procedure, 19.

Procure, *v.* procure, 127. See note,
p. 83.

Proigne, Progne (turned into a swallow), 55.

Prolixitee, prolixity, 18.

Proyne, 1 *pr. pl.* preen, trim our wings,
64. J.

Prye, *v.* pry, peer, gaze about, 72.

Purchace, *v.* obtain, 59, 184.

Pure, poor, 99, 101.

Purpose, *s.* purpose, 158.

Puruait, *pp.* purveyed, provided, 23.

Purueyance, providence, 130, 192;
Puruiance, 176.

Pykit, *pp.* adorned, 7. Chaucer has
piketh, trims, C. T. 9885; see Way's
note in Prompt. Parv., p. 397.

Pyne, *s.* pain, trouble, 155, 173, 175.
J.

Pynnit, *pp.* fastened, 180.

Quair, book, *title* (page 3). O. F.
quaier, spelt *quayer*, *cayer* in Cotgrave, mod. F. *cahier*, mod. E. *quire.*
See *Quire* in my Etym. Dict.

Quaking, *pres. pt.* shaking, 47.

Quhar, where, 17 ; Quhare, 58 ; Quhartill, whereunto, 170; Quhare [vn]to,
to what purpose, 68. J.

Quhele, *s.* wheel, 9, 159. See *quheill*
in additions to J.

Quhen, when, 2. J.

Quhich, which, 3. A bad form of
quhilk, which is the proper Northern
form.

Quhile, *s.* while, time, 2. J.

Quhilk, *pron.* which, 180 ; Quhilkis,
pl. 61. J.

Quhill, until, 108 ; whilst, p. 54, l. 12.

Quhilom, *adv.* once upon a time, formerly, 3 ; Quhilum, once, 88. J.

Quhirling, *s.* whirling, 165.

Quhirlit, *pp.* whirled, 189.

Quhislith, *pr. s.* whistles, 135.

Quhite, *a.* white, 46, 96.

Quho, *pron.* who, 57 ; whosoever, 78,
162, 182 ; As quho sais, as if one
should say, 77 ; Quhois, *gen.* whose,
56, 70.

Quhy, why, 81 ; *as sb.* reason why,
reason, 87, 93. J.

Quikin, *v.* quicken, 181.

Quit, *pp.* requited, 128 ; released, 6 ;
Quite, *as adj.* quit, 195. J.

Quoke, *pt. s.* quaked, 162. J.

Quyt, *imp. s.* requite, p. 54, l. 7.

Railit, *pp.* railed, 31.

Rancoure, ill will, 117.

Range, *s.* range, 158.

Rase, 1 *pt. s.* rose, 11.

Ravin, *a.* ravenous, 157. J.

Rawe, *s.* row, 154 ; On rawe, in a
row, 90. J.

Recouerance, recovery, 87.

Recounsilit, *pp.* reconciled, restored to
their loves, 90.

Reconforting, *s.* comforting again, 176.
J.

Recure, *s.* recovery, 10, 95 ; Recouer,
5. J.

Red, *v.* read, 196.

Reder, *s.* reader, 194.

Reherse, rehearsal, 127.

Rele, *v.* roll, turn (it) round, 9 ; roll,
165. J.

Relesch, *v.* relax, assuage, 184. "*Relascher*, to slacken, ease, refresh, remit;" Cotgrave.

Relesche, *s.* relaxation, ease, 25, 150, 176. "*Relasche*, a relaxation, ease, rest, repose, refreshment, truce, intermission;" Cotgrave.

Remanant, *s.* remnant, 137, 171. *Remanand* in Barbour.

Remede, remedy, 69, 138. J.

Remufe, *v.* remove, be removed, 188.

Remyt, *s.* excuse, forgiveness, 195.

Renewe, *s.* renewal, 125. Cf. *reherse* = rehearsal.

Repaire, *s.* concourse, 77. J.

Report, narrative, 4. J.

Requere, *imper. s.* pray, ask, 195. "*Requerir*, to request, intreat, beseech;" Cotgrave.

Resident, *pres. pt.* dwelling, residing, 115.

Ressaue, *v.* receive, 123; Ressauen, *pr. pl.* receive, 145; Ressauit, *pp.* received, 52, 84.

Rethorike, *s.* rhetoric, 196.

Rethorikly, *adv.* rhetorically, 7.

Retrete, retreat, 96.

Retrograde, *a.* backward, 170.

Reule, *v.* rule, 15; Reulen, 194.

Reuth, *s.* pity, 137.

Rew, *v.* have pity (on), 63; *imp. s.* 101. J.

Reyne, rain, 116.

Riall, *a.* royal, 125, 157. J.

Ro, *s.* roe, 157.

Rody, *a.* ruddy, 1.

Rold, *pp.* rolled, 163.

Rong, *pt. pl.* rang, 33.

Ronne, *pp.* run, 108; Bludy ronne, run over with blood, 55.

Rose, *s.* the rose, emblem of beauty, 186. See note. p. 92.

Rought, *pt. s.* recked, 27. See *Roucht* in J.

Rout, *s.* troop, shoal, 153.

Rowm, *a.* roomy, spacious, 77. A.S. *rûm*, adj. J.

Rude, rood, cross, 139. J.

Rudenes, rudeness, 49.

Rut, *s.* root, p. 54, l. 3.

Ruyne, ruin, 28.

Ryf, rife, common, 121.

Ryght[e], *a.* direct, 75.

Rynnis, *pr. s.* runs, passes, 171. J.

Rynsid, *pt. s.* rinsed, laved, purified, 1.

Sable, *s.* sable, 157.

Said, said (?), 125. But perhaps an error for *sad*, i.e., grave, serious.

Sall, 1 *pr. s.* shall, must, 43, 45; 2 *pr. s.* shalt, 128. J.

Salute, 1 *pt. s.* saluted, 98.

Sanctis, *pl.* saints, 191. J.

Saphire, sapphire, 46.

Sauf, safe; Hir worschip sauf, save her honour, 143.

Saulis, *pl.* souls, 123. J.

Schape, *v.* prepare, provide, 69. J.

Schede, *pp.* shed, 117.

Schene, *a.* bright, 95, 107, 110. J. A.S. *scéne.*

Schet, 1 *pt. s.* shut, 8. J.

Schill, *a.* shrill, 66. J.

Schire, *a.* clear, bright, shining, 76. J.

Schuldris, *pl.* shoulders, 96, 160. J.

Schupe, *pt. s.* shaped, destined, 24. So in Barbour.

Scole, *s.* scull, head, 7. Not 'school,' as Tytler supposed. "Cranium, *scolle*;" Wright's Vocabularies, vol. i. p. 179, l. 5.

Secretee, secrecy, 97.

See, *s.* sea, 22.

Seildin, *adv.* seldom, 9. J.

Seis, 2 *pr. s.* seest, 54, 86.

Sek-cloth, sack-cloth, 109. J. has *sek*, sack; from Icel. *sekkr.*

Seke, *a.* sick, ill, 58.

Sekirnesse, security, 71; Sekernesse, 5; Sekernes, 174. J.

Seknesse, sickness, 111.

Self, *s.* same material, 161.

Sely, *a.* seasonable, fit, 185; innocent, simple, 134; poor, miserable, 14, 44, 169. See *seily, sely* in J. A.S. *sælig.*

Sen, *conj.* since, 13, 26, 38, 57, 144. J.

Senatoure, senator, 3.

Sene, *v.* to see, 178.

Sentence, opinion, 149. So in Chaucer.

Septre, sceptre, 107.

Seruand, servant, 113; Seruandis, *pl.* 86, 184.

Seruis, service, 119.

Set, *v.* set, appoint, 38; Setten, *v.* set, bind, 37; Set, *pt. s.* placed, 5.

Sew, *imp. s.* follow, p. 54, l. 4.

Seyne, *v.* say, 27, 38, 42, 98.

Shapith, *imp. pl.* shape ye, provide, 102. This use of the plural implies respect.

Signifere, the zodiac (lit. sign-bearer), 76. J.

Signis, *pl.* signs of the zodiac, 76.

Sike, *v.* sigh, 44. J.

Simplese, *s.* simpleness, 194. (Better *simplesse.*)

Sitt, *pr. s.* sitteth, 196. So in Chaucer.

Slake, *v.* cease (lit. slacken), 161.

Slawe, *a.* slow, 155. J.

Sleuth, sloth, 119. J.

Slokin, *v.* slake, quench, 69, 168. J.

Sloppare, *a.* slippery, 163. J. has *slippar.*

Sluggart, *s.* sluggard, 58.

Slungin, *pp.* slung, cast, 165.

Smaragdyne, *s.* emerald, 155. Properly an adjectival form; from Lat. *smaragdus.*

Smertis, *pr. s.* pains, 141. So in Chaucer.

Snawe, snow, 67. J.

So, that; Quhen so, when that, 118,

Socoure, succour, 100.

Sodayn, *a.* sudden, 40.

Sodaynlye, *adv.* suddenly, 11; Sodeynly, 126.

Soiurne, *s.* sojourn, abode, 113.

Solemp[ni]t, *pp.* solemn, 79.

Sone, *voc.* son, 149.

Sone, soon, 75.

Song, *pp.* sung, 54.

Sonne, sun, 110.

Sore, *s.* grief, 182.

Soun, *s.* sound, 13, 152. So in Chaucer.

Soyte, *s.* suit, livery, 64.

Spangis, *pl.* spangles, 47. J.

Spede, *v.* succeed, 70; help, assist (see note), 28; Speid, succeed, 186. J.

Spede, *s.* success, 113. J.

Spere, sphere, 76. J.

Sperk, spark, 48.

Spottis, *pl.* spots, 161.

Sprad, *pt. pl.* spread, 21.

Springis, *pr. pl.* spring, bud forth, grow, 119.

Spurn, *v.* stumble, 185. See *Sporne* in J.

Squerell, *s.* squirrel, 155.

Stage, rank, place, 79.

Stale, *s.* a prison, 169. J. The same word as *stall.* See below.

Stallit, *pp.* placed, 170.

Standar, *a.* always standing, 156. See note, p. 87. This use of the form in *-ar* (E. *-er*) as adjectival is imitated from Chaucer's Assembly of Foules, where we find 'the *bilder* ook,' and 'the *shooter* ew.'

Stant, *pr. s.* stands, 167; consists, 15. So in Chaucer.

Starf, *pt. s.* died, 139. See Steruen.

Steik, *imp. s.* shut, p. 54, l. 17.

Stellifyit, *pp.* made into a star, 52. So in Chaucer. J.

Stent, 1 *pt. s.* stopped, 5; *pt. pl.* ceased, 35. J.

Stere, helm, 195; control, guidance, 130. J.

Stere, *v.* steer, guide, 194. J.

Stereles, *a.* without a helm, 15. From Chaucer.

Sterre, star, 99; Sterres, *pl.* 1.

Steruen, *v.* die, 102. See Starf. J.

Stond, *v.* stand, 88.

Stound, *s.* time, 53; hour, 118. J.

Stramp, *imp. s.* tramp, trample, p. 51, l. 19. (It can hardly be right; see note, p. 96).

Stranger, *adv.* more severely, 68. J. has *strang.*

Strangest, strongest, 149.

Straucht, *adv.* straight, 158; Straught, 126, 151. J.

Strayte, *a.* strict, 25. See *Strat* in J.

Strenth, strength, 71. J.

Strowit, *pp.* strewn, 65.

Styntith, *pr. pl.* cease, 118; Stynt, 1 *pt. s.* ceased, 53, 104; Stynten, 1 *pt. s.* (a false form, see note), 117. J.

Suete, *a. as sb.*, happiness, 182.

Sue[ue]nyng, *s.* dreaming, 174. See *Sweuin* in J. From A.S. *swefen.*

Sufficiante, *a.* sufficient, 183.

Suffisance, sufficiency, enough, 6, 16, 26.

Suffise, *v.* endure, 140.

Suich, such, 11.

Suith, *s.* truth, p. 53, l. 12.

Suld, *pt. s.* should, 15. J.

Suoun, in a swoon (orig. a pp. = A.S. *swogen*), 73. See *Swoon* in my Etym. Dict.

Superlatiue, *a.* most excellent, 197.

Supplye, *s.* supply, aid, help, 15, 112.

Surcote, *s.* upper garment, 160. "*Surcot,* an upper kirtle, or garment worn over the kirtle;" Cotgrave. Quite distinct from the use of the word given in J.

Surmounting, *pres. pt.* aspiring, 87.

Suspect, *pp.* suspected, 137.

Suth, *s.* truth, 137. J.

Syne, *adv.* afterwards, 192. J.

Tabartis, *pl.* tabards, cloaks, *i.e.*, clothing of feathers, 110. Cf. 'Birds of a feather flock together.' Chaucer has *tabard.*

Take, *pp.* taken, 90; Tak, 193.

Takenyng, *s.* taken, 176.

Takin, token, 118; Takyn, 41, 180. J.

Thame, them, 78.

Than, *adv.* then, 4, 63. J.

The, *pron. acc.* thee, 15, 129; *dat.* to thee, 106.

Theffect, the effect, the result, 141. So in Chaucer.

Theire, *error for* Thir, those, 6.

There as, where that, 113.

Thesiphone, Tisiphone (one of the furies); *by error for* Terpsichore (one of the muses), 19.

Thidderwart, thitherwards, 185. J.

Thilke, that, 5, 119.

Thir, *pron.* those, 56, 79, 104; these, 10, 51. In st. 6 read *thir* for *theire*. J.

Tho, *pron.* those, 39, 88, 144. Wrongly explained as "these" in J.

Tho, then, 12, 67; As tho, as at that time, 2. J.

Thraldom, servitude, 183; Thraldome, 28. See *Thrillage* in J.

Thrall, slave, 41; prisoner, 38; Thrallis, *pl.* thralls, 39.

Thrawe, *s.* time, short time, little while, 35, 45, 67. J.

Thrist, thirst, 69. J.

Throu, *prep. as v.* (go) through, penetrate, 63.

Throwe, *v.* drive, 17.

Tidingis, *pl.* tidings, 162.

Tiklyng, *s.* tickling, light motion, 21.

Tippit, *pp.* tipped, 157.

Tissew, *s.* thin (white) under-garment, 49. Cotgrave gives *tissu* in the sense of a "head-band of woven stuffe."

To, *prep.* for, 116; To mynd, to my remembrance, 2; To suich delyte, for such a delight, so delightful, 49.

To, too, 61.

To cum, to come, future, 14. Written *tocum.*

Tofore, *prep.* before, 103. J.

Tofore, *adv.* beforehand, 1, 2, 119. J.

To-forowe, *adv.* before, 23, 49; heretofore, 105.

To-gider, together, 124; Togidder, 68. J.

Tolter, *a.* tottery, unstable, 9; *adv.* unsteadily, 164. See *Totter* in my Etym. Dict.

Tong, language, 7.

Toure, tower, 40.

Toward, *prep.* as regards, 46.

Towardis, towards, 104.

To-wrye, *v.* turn, twist about, 164.

Wrongly given in J. under *Wry.* It is obviously a compound verb, with the prefix *to-*; cf. "distorqueo, ic *tó-wríthe*," Ælfric's Glossary, ed. Zupitza, p. 155.

Traist, *v.* trust, 130. J.

Translate, *v.* transform, change, 8.

Trauaile, *s.* toil, 69, 70.

Trauaile, *v.* travel, toil, 16; I *pr. s.* toil, 70.

Trauerse, screen, 90; Trevesse, 82. J.

Tressis, *pl.* tresses, 1.

Trety, treatise, 18. J.

Trevesse; see Trauerse.

Trowe, I *pr. s.* trow, believe, 36; 2 *pr. pl.* 11.

Tueyne, *a.* two, 42, 75.

Tuke, I *pt. s.* took, 13, 124.

Turment, *s.* torment, 19.

Turture, *s.* turtle-dove, 177. J.

Twiggis, *pl.* twigs, 54.

Twinklyng, *s.* twinkling, 163.

Twise, *error for* Twiës (*dissyllabic*), twice, 25.

Twistis, *pl.* twigs, 33, 119. J.

Twynklyng, *pres. pt.* twinkling, 1. But it is rather to be taken as put for *twynklen,* pr. pl. (they) twinkle.

Tyde, *s.* time, 160.

Tyme, time; Be tyme, betimes, in good time, 122.

Vale, *v.* descend, 172. Short for *avale.* Cotgrave has "*avaller,* to let, put, lay, cast, fell down, to let fall down."

Variance, *s.* contradiction, 161.

Variant, *a.* varying, variable, 137. J.

Vere, spring, 20. J.

Verray, *a.* true, 5; *adv.* very, 169.

Vertew, power, 74; Vertu, powerful influence, 20.

Vexit, *pp.* vexed, 174.

Vgly, *a.* ugly, 162.

Viage, voyage, 15. J.

Virking, *s.* working, influence, control, 188. Bad spelling of *wirking.*

Visioun, *s.* vision, 175.

Vmbre, *s.* shadow, shade, 134. J.

Vnaffraid, *a.* un-afraid, fearless, 35.

Vncouth, *pp.* unknown, 63, 66, 113.

Vncouthly, *adv.* strangely, 9.

Vnderstond, *pp.* understood, 127. Chaucer has *vnderstonde* (with final *e*) as a *pp.* in C. T. 4940.

Vndertake, *pp.* undertaken, 63. Short for *vndertaken;* the form is Southern; the Northern form is *vndirtan* (Barbour).

Vnicorne, *s.* unicorn, 155.

Vnknawin, *pp.* unknown, 105; *ill spelt* Vnknawing, it being unknown (to me), 45.

Vnknyghtly, *a.* unknightlike, disgraceful, 55.

Vnnethis, *adv.* scarcely, 98. See *uneith* in J.

Vnquestionate, unquestioned, 125.

Vnrypit, unripened, 14.

Vnsekernesse, insecurity, 15.

Vnsekir, *a.* insecure, 6. See *unsikker* in J.

Voce, voice, 74, 83. J.

Void, *a.* empty, 164.

Voidis, *pr. s.* dispels, 155. " *Vuider,* to void, evacuate, empty, exhaust, dispatch, make an end of;" Cotgrave.

Vre, fortune, luck, hap, 10. J. See my Glossary to Barbour's Bruce. O. F. *eur,* from Lat. *augurium.*

Vschere, usher, door-keeper, 97.

Vtrid, *pp.* uttered, 132. See note. Chaucer has the infin. *uttren,* C. T. 16302.

Wag, *v.* move, shake, 60.

Waile, *v.* bewail, 122.

Wald, 1 *pt. s.* would, 11; 2 *pt. s.* wouldst, 167; *pt. s.* would, 160; *error for* Nald, would not (see note), 140. J.

Walk, *v.* walk, 177.

Walking, *pres. pt.* waking, 173. J.

Walowit, *pp.* withered, p. 54, l. 11. See note, pp. 95, 96.

Wan, *pt. s.* won, 5.

Wandis, *pl.* rods, 31. Cf. *wand,* a fishing-rod, in J.

Wanting, *s.* lack, loss, 86.

Wantis, 2 *pr. s.* lackest, 169; *pr. s.* lacks, 15. Spelt *vantis* in Barbour.

Ward, *s.* ward, guardianship, 25.

Ware, *a.* wary, 164. Better *war,* as in Barbour.

Warld, world, 26, 122; great number, 82; Warldis, *gen.* world's, 3. J.

Warldly, *a.* worldly, mortal, 44, 51. J.

Wate, 2 *pr. s.* knowest, 129; *pr. s.* knows, 60. "Thou *vait,*" thou knowest, occurs in the Complaint of Scotland; see J., s.v. *Wait.*

Wawis, *pl.* waves, 16, 24, 100. J.

Wayke, *a.* weak, 14, 148. See *Waik* in J. Icel. *veikr.*

Wede, *s.* weed, garment, robe, 81. See *weed* in J.

Wedowis, *s. gen.* widow's, 156. J. See note, p. 87.

Weill, *s.* wealth, riches, p. 54, l. 3. See Wele.

Wele, *adv.* well, 14, 53, 64; Wele is him, it is well for him, 133. Cf. " *Well* is thee;" and see *Wele is* in J.

Wele, *s.* weal, 39; good fortune, 169. J.

Weltering, *pres. pt.* rolling, 24; tossing, 100. J.

Weltering, *s.* rolling, 163.

Werdes, *pl.* weirds, fates, lots, 9; Werdis, *gen. pl.* of fates, 169. J.

Were, *pt. subj.* were, 22; would be, 53, 143.

Werely, *a.* warlike, bristling, 155. J. gives two other examples of the sense 'warlike'; but not this one.

Werit, *pt. s.* wore, 160. Chaucer has *werede,* C. T. 75.

Weye, *v.* weigh, 120. Read, 3*e aughten maist weye,* ye ought most to weigh, *or* regard, *or* pay heed to.

Wight, *s.* wight, person, 42, 140. See *Wicht* in J.

Will, *pr. s.* desires, 106; Will thame translate, wants to transform itself, 8. *Eche estate* is taken as having a plural force.

Wilsum, *a.* wandering, straying, 19. See *Wilsum* in J. (given under *Will*); and see *Will of red* in Barbour.

Wirken, *v.* afflict, 68. See *Wark* in J.

Wise, *s.* way, 117; manner, 97. So in Chaucer.

Wist, 1 *pt. s.* knew, 76; 2 *pt. s.* knewest, 14. See Witt. (I think examples of *thou wist* are scarce.)

With, *prep. used in close connection with a verb*; Gouerne with my will, govern my will with, 16; Hir with to glad, to gladden her with, 190 (cf. 174); To schorten with thy sore, to shorten thy pain with, 111.

Witt, *v.* know, be aware, 128. See Wate, Wist. J.

Woke, 1 *pt. s.* woke, 174.

Wolf, *s.* wolf, 157.

Womanhede, womanhood, 117.

Wonder, *adv.* wonderfully, very, 96. See *Wondir* in Barbour.

Wonne, *pp.* won, 34. See Wan.

Worschip, *s.* honour, 136, 142. J.

Wortis, *pl.* herbs, 156.

Wote, 1 *pr. s.* wot, know, 47; *pr.*

knows, 44; Wostow, 2 *pr. s.* thou dost know, 59. See Wate.

Wrangit, *pp.* wronged, 92. J.

Wrechit, *a.* wretched, 167.

Wrest, *pp.* wrested, tortured, 10. A.S. *wrǽstan.*

Wrething, *s.* turning, changing of fortune, 146. See Writh.

Wring, *v.* wring the hands, lament, 57.

Writh, *v.* turn about, govern, wield, direct (lit. writhe), 107; turn aside, remove, 122. Most likely the author was thinking of Chaucer's tr. of Boethius, bk. 5, prose 3, where we find: "for yif that they myghten *wrythen* awey in other manere than thei ben purueyed," *i.e.,* for if things could be turned about (so as to fall out) in another manner from that which they were intended or foreseen, &c.

Writt, *v.* write, 182.

Wroght, *pp.* wrought, made, 77.

Wrokin, *pp.* wreaked, avenged, 69. J.

Wrye; On wrye, awry, aside, 73. *On wry* is in Barbour's Bruce, iv. 705.

Wyle, wile, plan, device, 2.

Wyre, wire, 1.

Wyte, *ger.* blame, 90. See note. J.

Y-, *prefix; the same as* I-, *prefix,* which see. Examples are Y-bete, Y-bought, Y-callit, Y-like, Y-thrung-in, Y-wallit, where Y-bete is in the infinitive mood, and Y-like is an adverb.

Ybete, *v.* beat, fall heavily, 116.

Ybought, *pp.* bought, 36.

Ycallit, *pp.* called, 170.

Ylike, *adv.* alike, 70.

Ymagynit, *pp.* imagined, 13.

Ympnis, *pl.* hymns, 33. See Impnis. J.

Ythrungin, *pp.* pushed together, thrust (upwards), 165. Given in J., s.v. *Thring.*

Ywallit, *pp.* walled, 159.

ʒa, yea, verily, 68. See *Ya* in J.

ʒalow, yellow, 95.

ʒate, *s.* gate, 125.

ʒelde, 1 *pr. s.* yield, 52.

ʒeris, *pl.* years, 22.

ʒit, yet, 63.

ʒok, *s.* yoke, 192.

ʒond, *adv.* yonder, 57. See *Yound* (better *Yond*) in J.

ʒone, *a.* yon, that, 88; those, 83.

ʒong, *a.* young, 7.

ʒoure alleris, of you all, 113. See note p. 81.

ʒouth, youth, 6.

REMARKS UPON JAMIESON'S DICTIONARY.

A few quotations from the Kingis Quair (apparently Tytler's edition) are given in full in Jamieson's Dictionary; but the number of words which occur in the poem, and are not in the Dictionary at all, or are not there given *in the same sense*, is rather large. I have observed the following, some of which are so simple as hardly to be worth notice; still, I give the list in full, including words which, though given, are wrongly or insufficiently explained. Abandon (not in this sense), alblastrie (insufficiently explained), anewis (the same), aspert (the sense given is not right), aworth (given rightly, but with a doubt), coppin (given by error for *croppin*, *coppin* being a false form), defade (omitted), dert (quite wrongly explained), embroudin (omitted), fantise (the sense 'vain appearance' should be omitted), fatoure (om.), fell (om. in this sense), foringit (wrongly inserted for *foriugit*), foriugit (om.), forwalowit (wrong), fret (om.), gesserant (not explained), herbere (wrong), herknere (om.), keye (om.), lesty (om.), list, *s.* (om.), lokin (om.), marciall (om.), met (om., unless *mete* be wrongly explained), one (om.), ourehayle (om.), oure-straught (om.), out of (om.), pace, *s.* (om. in this sense), pas *or* pace, *v.* (om. in this sense), pall (om.), part, *v.* (om.), party (om. in this sense), plyte (om.), poetly (om.), porpapyne (om.), pouert (om.), poure (om.), prime (om.), process, *s.* (om.), pyke (om. in this sense), quhirl (om.), quhisle (om.), quho (om.), quikin (om.), recouerance (om.), recounsilit (om.), relesch, *v.* (om.), relesche, *s.* (om.), remyt, *s.* (om.), renewe, *s.* (om.), report, *s.* (om.), rethorike (om.), rody (om.), rynsid (om.), secretee (om.), sike (here J. is *right*, but Tytler's quoted opinion is *wrong*), simplesse (om.), sloppare (om.), smert, *s.* (om.), soun (only given as *sowne*), soyte (om.), sperk (om.), strow, *v.* (om.), thilke (om.), tho (wrong; it means 'those'), toforowe (om.), tolter (wrong, it is not a *verb*), towardis (om.), translate (om.), vertew (not in this sense), vncouth (only given as *unco*), vnsekernesse (om.), void, *v.* (om.), vtrid, *from* uttir, *v.* (om.), wail, *v.* (om.), want, wanting (om.), weye (om.), womanhede (om.), wonder, *adv.* (om.), wortis (om.), wrechit (om.), wring, *v.* (om.), wrething (om.), writh (om.), wry (wrong), ybete (om.), зis (only given as *yhis*), зon (only given as *yhone*). In several cases, the etymologies in J. need revision; thus *abate* is not of Scandinavian origin; *axis* is O. French *acces*, and unrelated to *ache*; *chamlotte* has no connection with *camel*; *fere*, a companion, has no connection with F. *foire*, a fair; *fery* has no connection with A.S. *feorh*; *fonde* is A.S. *fandian*, not *fundian*; *proyne* is from F. *provigner*, which J. sets aside; *schene* is not allied to *shine*, nor G. *schön* to G. *scheinen*; neither *wait* nor *wis* are infinitives. There are cases in which a quotation from the Kingis Quair might be added; *e.g.*, under *traverse*, *welter*, *werely*, *wrest*. I venture to make these remarks because some of my corrections for the examples of words in Barbour have received attention, though a few were missed—viz., *allryn*, *assouerit*, *beleif*, *belene*, *betane*, &c.

Printed in the United States
102115LV00005B/66/A

9 781432 543556